JESUS, SYMBOL-MAKER FOR
THE KINGDOM

Jesus, Symbol-Maker for the Kingdom

BERNARD BRANDON SCOTT

FORTRESS PRESS   Philadelphia

Library of Congress Cataloging in Publication Data

Scott, Bernard Brandon, 1941-
　　Jesus, symbol-maker for the kingdom.

　　Includes index.
　　1. Jesus Christ—Parables. 2. Kingdom of God.
3. Religion and language. I. Title.
BT375.2.S35　　226′.806　　　80-2388
ISBN 0-8006-0654-X　　　　　AACR2

8578A81　Printed in the United States of America　1–654

For Marilyn,
the leaven in my life

CONTENTS

INTRODUCTION

A wise beginning for any large inquiry is to entertain the
postulate that reality, or a goodly part of it, is not obvious
and discoverable by overt public methods of investigation, but is latent, subtle and shy.

—Philip Wheelwright

Some times are propitious for beginnings, for asking new questions of old tasks, for returning to problems that never can be
solved. Such a time may be upon us as regards the quest for the
historical Jesus. The signs of the times indicate that we should
try again, despite Albert Schweitzer's warning that the Jesus we
reconstruct may reflect only our own desires.

In the 1950s and '60s a movement arose espousing both the
theological legitimacy and historical possibility of a New Quest.
Coupled with a New Hermeneutic, it appeared to offer progress,
but gradually it died out and disappeared. No fundamentally
new vision of Jesus emerged.

And yet it was not fruitless. One aspect has remained and
continues to generate interest especially in this country. Latter-
day parable researchers are heirs of the New Quest and New
Hermeneutic. Amos Wilder and Robert Funk infused into this
tradition the methods of literary criticism. Wilder's *Early Christian Rhetoric* and Funk's *Language, Hermeneutic, and the Word
of God* represent the emergence of a distinctly American perspective. This accent continues with the work of Dan O. Via
and John Dominic Crossan. Parables became the locus of Jesus
research.

This book consciously works out of that legacy and seeks to
expand it beyond the confines of parables to other forms of

Jesus' language. The literary, structuralist models developed in parable criticism provide a basis for attempting a coherent insight into Jesus' language as a whole. The accent upon language distinguishes our task from previous ventures at understanding the historical Jesus. Language is not equivalent to his "words," but a system of signs. His individual utterances and deeds are performances playing upon the potential of his language. As such, individual sayings imply a system of signs. By analogy, a sentence as performance implies undergirding structures, one aspect of which is syntax whose rules can be deduced from the examples of a number of performances. Thus, Jesus' utterances can be explored so as to deduce a grammar of their symbolic organization.

Norman Perrin's classification of Kingdom as symbol represents a major development in contemporary scholarship. In chapter 1 we will review the discussion on Kingdom to highlight the significance of, and remaining problems with, Perrin's understanding. Kingdom as symbol will serve as a hypothesis to guide our study. Language of Jesus that modifies the presiding symbol, Kingdom, should exhibit the tensive characteristics necessary to refract a symbol. Recent parable scholarship has exploited such language, especially in the understanding of parable as metaphor.

Since parables are performances of Jesus' language, in chapters 2 and 3 we will describe discursively the underlying phenomenal world of parable, i.e., the horizon of meaning of which these parables are particular expressions. To understand parables as performances we need to read them in such a way that what makes the performance possible is made clear. In reading parables, we want to describe the phenomenal world supporting them. To do that we will develop a series of theses that present prominent features of that supporting world. Our method is deductive; from the parables as performances we seek the undergirding grammar or structure.

But because we follow a deductive method seeking what is underneath, we risk the danger of mistaking our deductions for the parable. Therefore our procedure attempts to keep the actual performances of Jesus' language always before us by constantly testing our deductions against the actual text. This creates a circular movement wherein we repeatedly return to the surface expression.

After developing a descriptive analysis of Jesus' language, we will formalize in chapter 4 that phenomenal world by means of models. This chapter is the most theoretical and abstract, and yet critical, for formal models indicate how Jesus' language as a system of signs effects meaning in the parables as individual performances. Just as sentence diagramming explains how a sentence effects meaning, so our models explain how parables effect meaning.

But if we can isolate a grammar for parables, how does that grammar relate to other forms of Jesus' language? In chapter 5 we will use our models to analyze a selected group of sayings and deeds: do these sayings and deeds result from the same organizing symbolic world as parables? We will concentrate on aspects that have remained unanswered in traditional research because the test of any new method is its ability to solve previous problematics.

We begin by accepting as a hypothesis Perrin's classification of Kingdom as symbol. In chapter 6 we will revisit the hypothesis not only to clarify further what is meant by symbol but even more to understand how Kingdom as symbol functions in Jesus' language. How do his language and its presiding symbol Kingdom of God refract and interact with each other?

Two assumptions underlie this effort. Because what we want to talk about is essentially unspeakable in discursive language, we have adopted insight as a methodological principle. In chapter 1 the significance of this principle will become clear. Secondly, we are taking a sounding, digging a test hole into Jesus' language. Our study makes no claim to be exhaustive in either what it has to say or in the material covered. It does claim that the material selected is representative of the authentic Jesus material. It is also, I believe, the first attempt to mount a literary analysis of the historical Jesus' language across formal lines.

To deal with the historical Jesus is to also deal with the thought of a great many thinkers. But two men in particular need to be singled out: Rudolf Bultmann and Norman Perrin.

Both have left their stamp upon the scholarly study of synoptic material. There are points at which I disagree with them; nevertheless I consider myself to be their student. In this country, Perrin is an especially important link between Bultmann and certain distinctive characteristics of American scholarship.

It is a great privilege to thank those who have made this study possible. The Board of Overseers of St. Meinrad set the sabbatical policy that granted me the freedom to complete this study. Fr. Daniel Buechlein, President of the School of Theology, was generous in his support of the project. Three of my colleagues gave more encouragement and help than they will ever know: David Buttrick, Juliana Casey, and Colman Grabert. Without such friends the intellect would soon wither away. Leander Keck and Robert Funk were generous with their time in reading the manuscript. I owe special thanks to John Hollar of Fortress Press for his encouragement. Shirley Risinger's dedication in deciphering my typescript went beyond a job to the level of craft. Finally, my wife has requested that I not say those things about her that the form "Author's Introduction" demands; I won't, but that does not mean they are not true.

1

CONVERGENCE OF HORIZONS: KINGDOM AND PARABLE

Jesus ties parables to Kingdom of God by using the former to describe the latter. In modern scholarship both have developed their own momentum as research topics. At the beginning of this century both were involved in charting an eschatological interpretation of Jesus, but Johannes Weiss and Albert Schweitzer pursued the topic of Kingdom while Adolf Jülicher overturned the allegorical interpretation of parables.[1] Both topics have figured prominently in various reconstructions of the historical Jesus,[2] and yet the estrangement has continued.

In recent years both topics have witnessed intense activity. Norman Perrin's work on Kingdom of God and Robert Funk and Dan Via's on parables come immediately to mind.[3] But, as in the beginning, there is similarity and difference. All three scholars have used literary criticism to inject new life into old debates. But Perrin has built upon the work of Weiss and Schweitzer, while Funk and Via have followed upon Jülicher.

This recent work has laid a foundation from which to reexamine the relation of parable and Kingdom. Perrin's analysis of Kingdom as symbol and Funk's of parable as metaphor provide the methodological possibility of viewing Jesus' language as a unified system. The centrality of Kingdom in Jesus' teaching and the parables' close relation to it demand an effort to underline their unity. Such is our task in this work. In this chapter we will review recent scholarship on Kingdom and parables to expose clues that will allow their interrelatedness to appear.

5

THE KINGDOM OF GOD

Modern scholarship has reached a consensus that Jesus' teaching is centered or summed up in his preaching of the Kingdom of God.[4] Of that there is little doubt today. Yet despite its centrality, one of the synoptic tradition's anomalies is that the meaning of Kingdom of God is assumed, not explicated, in that tradition.[5] This has caused untold difficulties in the history of interpretation as scholars have sought for an appropriate Jewish background against which to understand Jesus' usage.

In the spread of resulting options, two examples can serve as illustrations. Hermann Samuel Reimarus, writing at the beginning of the quest, saw precisely the problem of the non-definition of Kingdom of God in the New Testament and concluded that its meaning must have been clear to all. Therefore to determine Jesus' intention, one only need discover its usual meaning in first-century Judaism.[6] Reimarus's examination of Jewish texts convinced him that a political messiah was expected. This messiah would establish a temporal kingdom in Jerusalem, "whereby he would free them of all servitude and make them masters over other peoples."[7]

Albert Schweitzer, from an overview of available options, seized upon the apocalyptic mentality of postexilic Judaism and identified the Kingdom of God with the notion of the new age to come. For Schweitzer, Kingdom was an eschatological, apocalyptic term denoting the world's end. Thus Jesus became an apocalyptic preacher of the impending end.[8]

Both views are extreme and would be rejected today, but they graphically demonstrate the importance of the Jewish background as an interpretative tool for determining the meaning of Kingdom of God. Attempting to isolate a single, specific background has led scholarship off course. Is there a single background, or rather is the term itself polyvalent, open to different meanings?

Norman Perrin devoted a good part of his scholarly life to this topic. Because he was so conscious both of the evolution of scholarship and of his own thought, his research on the background of Kingdom of God clearly shows the available options. He produced three major works dealing with the Kingdom of God. The first, *The Kingdom of God in the Teaching of Jesus*,[9] is a summary of scholarship from Albert Schweitzer to the late 1950s. His *Rediscovering the Teaching of Jesus*[10] was a major historical exegesis attempting to authenticate the principal texts of Jesus dealing with Kingdom. The third, *Jesus and the Language of the Kingdom*,[11] pursues the investigation with a closer attention to the function of language, as the title suggests.

In concluding the first book, Perrin asked "Is the Kingdom of God an apocalyptic concept in the teaching of Jesus?"[12] The question's phrasing, generated by research into the history of scholarship, is important to observe. Kingdom of God first is classified within the worldview of apocalyptic and secondly as a concept. Because of the specific worldview (apocalyptic) through which Kingdom is understood, its meaning is determined not by Jesus' usage, but by the apocalyptic worldview. Secondly, as a *concept*, it functions as an ideational phenomenon with a specific and specifiable meaning. Perrin answers his question with an emphatic Yes! Kingdom of God is an apocalyptic concept in Jesus' teaching.[13]

This answer leads Perrin to raise a second question, concerning the Kingdom's temporality.[14] He notes the failed arguments of both Schweitzer and Weiss for the Kingdom's complete futurity, and also those of C. H. Dodd for its being wholly present.[15] Perrin himself maintains that Kingdom is both present and future, a commonly held position today.[16]

In his own analysis of Kingdom of God as an apocalyptic concept, Perrin presents a summary of the textual evidence.[17] With sure strokes he sketches the development of prophetic,[18] and then apocalyptic thought. For him, a chief characteristic of apocalyptic is an "eschatological dualism, the sharp distinction between the present age and the age to come."[19] The centering upon temporality identifies the *concept* of Kingdom with the *event* of the coming of the new age.[20] Thus, a concept has now unconsciously become a historical event. Perrin summarizes his discussion of apocalyptic expectation as follows: "The important point for our purposes is to note that this bewildering complex of expectation does, in fact, revolve around two central themes: God's decisive intervention in history and human experience, and the final state of the redeemed to which the intervention leads."[21]

Perrin then examines Kingdom of God as a specific term in apocalyptic literature. He argues that the specific usage agrees with the two points of his summary, but he makes the important observation that Kingdom of God "occurs only rarely—some 7 (9?) times in the whole range of the apocalyptic literature."[22] That it appears in apocalyptic literature is not to be denied, but its lack of frequency ought to lead us to question whether it ought to be identified exclusively with an apocalyptic concept, or whether it is plastic enough to receive an apocalyptic interpretation.

In the final section of this first work, Perrin touches upon those texts of Jesus in which Kingdom appears.[23] Of particular interest for our concern is Luke 17:20f, a text to which he returned a number of times.[24] In his exegesis, the Kingdom's arrival cannot be calculated in advance, nor will it be accompanied with apocalyptic signs because God's rule will come in a manner which only he can determine. The saying rejects a predetermined plan of history to which apocalyptic seers have access. "In effect, we have in this saying a rejection of the apocalyptic understanding of history and return to the prophetic understanding."[25] Perrin's own early study implicitly questions apocalyptic as an appropriate category for interpreting Kingdom of God in Jesus' teaching.

Rediscovering the Teaching of Jesus, the middle panel in Perrin's continuing triptych, marks an important shift in his thought. Bultmann's influence is much more evident, especially in the use of form criticism. But from the point of view of the question we are pursuing, Perrin represents little movement. While he still assumes that Kingdom in Jesus' teaching is an apocalyptic concept, that it is parallel to the apocalyptic notion of the age to come,[26] yet he sees that Jesus' linguistic usage is strange in a Jewish context.[27] For Jesus, Kingdom is a "reference to that state secured for the redeemed" by God's decisive intervention. Perrin continues, "In this he differs from Judaism, especially by making normative for his teaching the . . . usage which is rare and untypical in Judaism."[28]

But Perrin makes a real advance in understanding Jesus' sayings with a specific apocalyptic cast.[29] He concludes: "The first result of the investigation, then, is to establish major differences between Jesus and his contemporaries in that, although he spoke of the future, he gave neither specific form to his future expectation . . . nor did he express it in terms of specific time element."[30] There still remains for Perrin futurity in the teaching of Jesus (e.g., the Lord's Prayer, "thy Kingdom come"), but the apocalyptic form of futurity has been eliminated. His own analysis then questions identifying Kingdom of God as an apocalyptic concept of Jesus' teaching.

In his last major work on this topic, *Jesus and the Language of the Kingdom*, Perrin makes significant moves away from the problem's inherited formulation. He still takes for granted that the usage is derived from the world of apocalyptic,[31] but severe cracks have begun to appear. In dealing with the *Kaddish* he notes that "the form of the expectation expressed by the petition 'may he establish his kingdom' will have varied from individual to individual," although he still insists that the apocalyptic expectation would have predominated.[32] Also concerning the Kingdom's temporality, which we saw was generated by the apocalyptic assumption, Perrin asks "whether it is legitimate to think of Jesus' use of Kingdom of God in terms of 'present' and 'future' at all."[33]

In a most decisive gain, Perrin rejects "concept" as applied to Kingdom of God and adopts "symbol."[34] For him, Kingdom is now a religious symbol in Jesus' message, albeit a symbol derived from Jewish apocalyptic. He follows Philip Wheelwright's definition of a symbol: "A symbol, in general, is a relatively stable and repeatable element of perceptual experience, standing for some larger meaning or set of meanings which cannot be given, or not fully given, in perceptual experience itself."[35] In Wheelwright's understanding symbol is by definition contrasted with cognitive, conceptual experience. Symbols expose other dimensions of human experience. He makes this clear by distinguishing between what he calls steno-symbols and tensive symbols. A steno-symbol has a one-to-one relation with what it symbolizes. He uses the example, among others, of the mathematical symbol *pi*. Importantly, a steno-symbol's referent is knowable in ways other than through the symbol and is exhausted within the symbol. A tensive symbol, on the other hand, cannot be expressed by any one referent or (a point not noticed by Perrin) one whose referent itself is symbolic or not capable of complete capture.[36]

The identification of Kingdom as a tensive symbol in Jesus' language is an important moment in scholarship's history. With the rejection of Kingdom as a concept, Perrin is able to break the assumption that its meaning (referent) can be specified and is specifiable.[37] Furthermore, as a symbol referring to the story (myth) of God's activity among his people, it does not of necessity have to refer to a coming historical event. (It of course can, and Perrin shows how it sometimes does in apocalyptic literature.) It appeals to Israel's consciousness by symbolizing Yahweh's past dealings with his people.

Despite the gain, Perrin is still entrapped in the inherited question. The conclusion to his survey of Jewish usage makes this clear: "Indeed by the time of Jesus it had come to represent particularly the expectation of a final, eschatological act of God on behalf of his people."[38] Thus, Perrin still maintains his assumptions: (1) Kingdom of God is derived from the world of Jewish apocalyptic; (2) it is a major symbol within that tradition; and, (3) against this background Jesus' usage must be understood.

Perrin has undermined his own assumptions. The symbol's infrequency in Jewish apocalyptic and occurrence in other literature (e.g., the *Kaddish*) demonstrates that it does not have a steno-referent. Nor is it clear that the apocalyptic "new age" is a steno-symbol, comparable to the mathematical notion of *pi*. This reduces apocalyptic thought to banality. As Günter Klein has pointed out, Kingdom of God and new age do not have the same referent.[39] Apocalyptic is concerned with a new beginning, not with God's rule afterward. Kingdom of God as a symbol is open to elastic, plurisignificant meaning. It uses God's past dealings with his people as King to indicate how God deals with them now.

Ultimately, Perrin has fallen victim to a totally genetic mode of interpretation. His sketching of the symbol's history is too neat and clear. His analysis does show the symbol's plurisignificant and tensive character, but the referent is not a single apocalyptic concept or event. Because of the symbol's plurisignificance, Perrin's method of analysis is suggestive of meaning, not determinative.

THE KINGDOM AND PARABLES

I propose a somewhat different approach. To discover the referent which Kingdom of God symbolizes in Jesus' language demands a synchronic analysis, i.e., *Jesus' own language* must provide the clues. The first and most important clue is the simple observation that Jesus did not define Kingdom of God in discursive language.[40] This observation prompts the question as to why he did not offer such a definition, laying the basis for our second clue. One cannot respond that he offered no definition because it was commonly understood. If that were so, how does one explain the controversy and repeated requests for explanation? If its meaning were commonly understood, why has scholarship not been more successful in reconstructing the meaning? Finally, such an objection forgets that we are dealing with a symbol, not a concept.

When pressed to clarify his proclamation of the Kingdom, Jesus responded with parables.[41] From a synchronic perspective parables represent Jesus' choice of the most appropriate vehicle for understanding Kingdom of God. In order to achieve a unified insight into Jesus' message, the parables must be analyzed so as to focus their understanding of Kingdom in a precise fashion.

If the history of scholarship led to the conclusion that to analyze Kingdom one must begin with parables, likewise recent research on parables indicates the method to follow to achieve a unified insight. Such scholarship has explored parables as metaphor: they are not discursive and cannot be reduced to discursive speech without substantial loss of meaning. Parables refer to something other than themselves, ultimately Kingdom of God, which is itself a symbol with some other referent.

A diagram will help illustrate the situation.

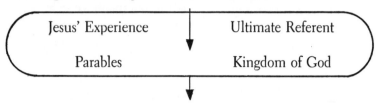

| Jesus' Experience | Ultimate Referent |
| Parables | Kingdom of God |

The vertical line stands for Kingdom of God's diachronic, i.e., historical, development. Within a general framework that diachronic usage can be established. The horizontal plane represents synchronic usage in Jesus' language.[42] His experience of the ultimate referent is expressed by the symbol Kingdom of God. The ultimate referent is not immediately available except symbolically. Jesus' attempt to clarify the symbol in turn generates parables. Parables relate to the ultimate referent metaphorically through the symbol Kingdom of God. A mutual relationship exists between the terms of the diagram. This diagram exposes the problematic of a purely historical (diachronic) understanding of Kingdom. Such an analysis is inadequate because in the speaker's judgment, it was inadequate from the beginning. The parables are an attempt to rectify that inadequacy.

If we seek an insight into Jesus' language through parables, that insight must be metaphorical. It cannot be reduced to discursive speech or propositions. The interpreter can attempt to draw out or provide the possibility of understanding, but one can never replace the original metaphor. To write a book about what cannot be written is to risk verbosity in the face of silence. Even though nonverbal, symbolic communication may be an eschatological goal, we have little choice but to work within our own verbal tradition. We now need to ask how parable can reveal these dimensions of Kingdom.

PARABLES AS METAPHOR

Certain elements about the parable qua parable make it finely attuned to its function of disclosing a symbol like Kingdom of God. C. H. Dodd proposed a classic definition of parable: "At its simplest the parable is a metaphor or simile drawn from nature or common life, arresting the hearer by its vividness or strangeness, and leaving the mind in sufficient doubt about its precise application to tease it into active thought."[43] The classification of parable as metaphor sparked a discussion which has provided the most important gain in recent parable research.[44] A review of this theoretical work on metaphor will indicate how parables can serve as a framework for understanding the symbol Kingdom of God in Jesus' language.

An important moment in the discussion is Robert Funk's analysis of "Parable as Metaphor" in his *Language, Hermeneutic, and the Word of God,*[45] which provides a theoretical understanding of metaphor. Funk modifies and clarifies Dodd's definition by distinguishing among simile, metaphor, and symbol. In simile the accent lies upon comparison: A is like B. The analogous relationship between A and B allows A to be illustrated in terms of B. Simile, for Funk, is primarily an illustrative, pedagogical instrument.[46] Metaphor, on the other hand, underplaying the element of comparison, states that A is B. While similarity between A and B suggests a relationship, Funk argues that a metaphor, "because of the juxtaposition of two discrete and not entirely comparable entities, produces an impact upon the imagination and induces a vision of that which cannot be conveyed by prosaic or discursive speech."[47]

Metaphor's formation is illogical in terms of discursive, ordinary speech. To say that A is B defies ordinary conventions of language.[48] By its very nature metaphor creates new meaning.[49] Meaning is contained in neither A nor B, but is effected in their juxtaposition.[50] In the case of parables this juxtaposition is especially important to notice. As a Jewish symbol, Kingdom is both known and unknown to the audience. Likewise for parable: its terms are known to the audience by means of its construction. But a parable's meaning as metaphor lies not in the story nor in a culture's understanding of Kingdom, but in the juxtaposition of parable and symbol.[51]

Also important for our concern are Funk's brief remarks on symbol as related to metaphor. Following Owen Barfield, Funk suggests that in symbolic language one speaks of B without mentioning A even though everyone knows A is the topic of discussion. "Symbolism is metaphor with the primary term suppressed."[52] In our case, Kingdom of God is B, while A is left unexpressed, suppressed. I would suggest that it is left unexpressed because it represents a reality so deep as to be unexpressible beyond the first expression, Kingdom of God.[53]

C. S. Lewis's distinction between the master's and pupil's metaphor further refines an understanding of metaphor.[54] A master's metaphor "is freely chosen, it is among many possible modes of expression."[55] This metaphor is used as a replacement for discursive thought or as a teaching technique for clarifying difficult concepts. Once grasped, a master's metaphor is no longer necessary and may actually hinder clarity of thought. To say that clouds are huge puffs of cotton suspended in air is a metaphor. It is used to lead to an unknown object (cloud) by means of a known object (cotton). If after the comparative element is seen the metaphor were maintained, it would mislead. Similarly, in the sentence "the ship plows the ocean," "plows" is metaphorical. Not intended to be taken literally, it serves to conjure up an appropriate vision of the activity. Another word (for example, "cuts") could be substituted without substantial loss of meaning.

Lewis's second type of metaphor, pupil's metaphor, "is not chosen at all; it is the unique expression of a meaning that we cannot have in any other terms; it dominates completely the thought of the recipient; his truth cannot rise above the truth of the original metaphor."[56] A pupil's metaphor cannot be done away with without substantial loss of meaning, for it is the unique path of entry to the metaphor's referent. For Funk and others, Jesus' parables are pupil metaphors.

Dominic Crossan has further developed an understanding of metaphor as poetic. A poetic metaphor attempts "to articulate a referent so new or so alien to consciousness that this referent can only be grasped within the metaphor itself."[57] Meaning is created within the metaphor. Metaphor creates a world of meaning into which a hearer is invited to enter. That world of metaphor then becomes the lens through which the hearer views his own world. Crossan raises two important observations: the primacy of metaphor itself and the importance of "world."

[Handwritten marginal note, left side, vertical:] But this is not a metaphor in the "creation of meaning" in the "creation of meaning" = mere lexical entity at this point.

Metaphor has the ability to direct attention to a referent not otherwise expressible in language, or as Kafka says, "All these parables merely mean the incomprehensible is incomprehensible."[58] This capability makes parable very suitable for disclosing religious symbols. Precisely the inability to capture in discursive speech such a reality underlines parable's significance as revealer and creator of experience.

Parable as metaphor demands the parable never be done away with. A parable's interpretation is always secondary and in no way necessary for parable. Insofar as an interpretation stands authoritatively in front, it closes off a parable's opening, violating what it is supposed to interpret. Allegorical interpretations laid upon the parables by successive generations of Christians run the risk of closing off the parable's hermeneutical potential and must first be removed if parable is to be parable.[59]

A parable's openness and primacy place limitations upon a modern interpreter. In seeking a unified insight we must be careful not to create one other than that disclosed by the parables themselves. A would-be interpreter may not impose or explain meaning. The true task is to provide an opportunity for meaning's disclosure by creating the necessary conditions for hearing. We cannot state what a parable means, for it has no meaning separate from itself. We can only circumscribe the terms necessary for hearing.

Parable as metaphor is generated from the experiential world of the teller.[60] Parables, expressing the incomprehensible in terms of the comprehensible, are developed out of Jesus' fundamental vision/experience of reality. Specifically for Jesus' parables, the experience which comes to expression is the experience of God as symbolized by Kingdom of God.

No one experiences anything in a void. With the experience is given the referential horizon that grants it meaning. To quote Ray Hart, "Why do some see the cow as a sacred object, while others see it as a beef-steak?"[61] Nothing about "cow" dictates it be worshiped or eaten. The referential horizon determines our perception and consequent understanding. The referential nexus constitutes the world of meaning into which the object or experience is fitted as a meaningful object or experience. Robert Funk, building upon Hart, defines world in this way: "The term 'world' in a phenomenological sense refers to the fundamental horizon or referential nexus within which consciousness apprehends and things are apprehended."[62]

Parables are semantizations or verbalizations of Jesus' World. They serve as referential nexus for Kingdom of God and Jesus' experience of God, as an attempt to create a World of meaning that grants a hearer the necessary World by which to hear and experience Kingdom. To enter the World of parable is to enter a new horizon that seeks to orient one to the expected object, Kingdom of God.

Parable as metaphorical World suggests a method whereby parables can be used to formulate our sought-after insight. Since parables both point through themselves to an experience and set the terms for that experience, can we delineate their horizon of meaning with any precision? On the one hand, we cannot. We cannot substitute some other phenomenon for parables. Such has been the burden of our argument. But can we develop a metalanguage (a language about language) that delineates that horizon of meaning? A principal thesis of this book is that such is possible. Following the analysis of each parable in chapters 2 and 3, a series of five theses will be proposed that seek in discursive language to indicate the horizon of the parable's World.

The purpose of this attempt must be clearly understood. Negatively, we are not seeking to discover Jesus' consciousness. Rather, our proposed theses have the status of a reference back to the parables themselves. Their value and purpose is to generate a conversation about parables that will in turn generate insight into parables. Thus the analysis of each parable will serve as an attempt to clarify further the referential nexus represented by the parable's World.

Parable's very metaphorical character justifies our procedure. While agreeing with Funk that a parable's meaning effect is created by the juxtaposition of the unexpected and with Crossan that juxtaposition can create a new World of meaning, nevertheless a metaphor's viability depends upon the commonality between referent and metaphor. Since the parable's referent is a symbol (i.e., disclosing a further referent), the hearer of the parable faces a difficult criterial problem. How does one judge the adequacy of the implied commonality? This is possible only if somehow in the act of disclosure the auditor can experience the referent! In the parables of Jesus this leads to a peculiar mechanism. Kingdom of God as symbol is both a known and an unknown phenomenon. Parable as metaphor will be judged by a hearer's knowledge/experience of the symbol as well as the metaphor's ability to convince the hearer that it discloses that reality more adequately than previous knowledge/experience. A hearer can reject the metaphor as inadequate or convert to the metaphor as revealing. Since parable demands judgment, our attempt to describe the terms of that judgment as a referential nexus or World is justified by parable itself.

INSIGHT AS METHOD

Our enterprise runs the risk of betraying itself by inadvertently reducing symbol and parable to discursive language or else mistaking our discussions for the parables. If this happens, we will suffer a loss of potential meaning. In an effort to prevent such a reduction, we have proposed the generation of a unified insight as our goal and have argued that parables as metaphor present the possibility of such an insight. It is now imperative to describe more fully what is meant by insight, as it has a methodological function in this study. According to Bernard Lonergan, insight "consists in a grasp of intelligible unity or relation in the data or image or symbol."[63] The data presented to consciousness is discrete, and intelligence organizes that data into intelligible wholes.[64] Insight results from inquiry and is cumulative. It is an intuitive grasp of a whole, and as such is preconceptual.[65] "It is the active ground whence proceed conception, definition, hypothesis, theory, system."[66]

Such an accumulation of insights is sought in this study. Because Kingdom of God is a tensive symbol, the appropriate manner for understanding this symbol is insight. How is that insight to be grasped? Through the parables as metaphors. Only when one begins to see the intelligible unity between symbol and parable and parables themselves, will one gain insight into Kingdom. The density of referent created by the conjunction of symbol and metaphor demands insight, but by its very character that insight will only be approximated in our discursive language.

The preconceptual nature of insight must be insisted upon. We are seeking that accumulation of insights that grounds the formulation of conception, definition, hypothesis, etc.

We now turn our attention in the next two chapters to a reading of eight parables. In these two chapters we are seeking to expose the phenomenal World of parables so as to generate those insights that will allow us in chapter 4 to develop formal models for a description of the parabolic World.

NOTES

1. Johannes Weiss, *Jesus' Proclamation of the Kingdom*, trans. Richard Hiers and David Holland, Lives of Jesus Series (Philadelphia: Fortress Press, 1971; first published 1892) and Albert Schweitzer, *The Quest of the Historical Jesus*, trans. W. Montgomery (New York: Macmillan Company, 1968; first published 1906). Both of these studies changed forever research on the Kingdom of God. Adolf Jülicher, *Die Gleichnisreden Jesu* (Darmstadt: Wissenschaftliche Buchgesellschaft, 1969; first published 1899–1910), attacked the allegorical interpretation of parables and began the modern course of study.

2. The use of "historical" is confusing and controversial. By "historical" I mean the Jesus the historian can investigate with his tools. Leander Keck, A *Future for the Historical Jesus* (1971; reprint ed., Philadelphia: Fortress Press, 1981), pp. 18–25, surveys the problems associated with the term. For a summary of recent scholarship on the historical Jesus, cf. Gustaf Aulén, *Jesus in Contemporary Historical Scholarship*, trans. Ingalill H. Hjelm (Philadelphia: Fortress Press, 1976). For a conservative evaluation of modern scholarship, cf. Charles C. Anderson, *Critical Quests of Jesus* (Grand Rapids: Eerdmans, 1969).

3. For references to Perrin's work see below notes 4, 9, and 10. Robert Funk, *Language, Hermeneutic and the Word of God*, hereinafter, *LHWG* (New York: Harper and Row, 1966); Dan O. Via, *The Parables* (Philadelphia: Fortress Press, 1967).

4. E.g., Norman Perrin, *Jesus and the Language of the Kingdom* (Philadelphia: Fortress Press, 1976), p. 1; Hans Conzelmann, *Jesus*, trans. Raymond Lord, intro. John Reumann (Philadelphia: Fortress Press, 1973), p. 51.

5. For Conzelmann, this indicates the term Kingdom of God maintains its Jewish substratum (*Jesus*, p. 68).

6. Hermann Samuel Reimarus, *Reimarus: Fragments*, ed. Charles Talbert, trans. Ralph Fraser, Lives of Jesus Series (Philadelphia: Fortress Press, 1970), pp. 123–24.

7. Ibid., p. 126.

8. *Quest*, pp. 330–97.

9. Norman Perrin, *The Kingdom of God in the Teaching of Jesus* (London: SCM Press, 1963).

10. Norman Perrin, *Rediscovering the Teaching of Jesus* (New York: Harper and Row, 1967).

11. See note 4 above.

12. *Kingdom of God*, p. 158.

13. Ibid., pp. 158–59.

14. Ibid.

15. C. H. Dodd, *The Parables of the Kingdom* (New York: Charles Scribner's Sons, 1961). This book was based upon the Shaffer Lectures at Yale University in 1935.

16. W. G. Kümmel, *Promise and Fulfillment*, trans. Dorothea M. Barton, Studies in Biblical Theology 23 (London: SCM Press 1957).

17. *Kingdom of God*, pp. 160–70. Perrin reviewed this material again in *Rediscovering*, pp. 54–60, and in *Jesus and the Language*, pp. 16–32. In each case the pattern is the same: prophetic develops into apocalyptic. There is never any consideration of the place of wisdom literature. Perrin's thought seems dominated in these surveys by a simple developmental model of history.

18. *Kingdom of God*, p. 160. Perrin acknowledges a great dependence upon von Rad's *Theology of the Old Testament, Kingdom of God*.

19. Ibid., p. 164.

20. In *Rediscovering*, p. 59, n. 7, Perrin traces this identification back to G. Dalman, *Words of Jesus*, written at the turn of the century. Actually, Schweitzer and others had made the same identification that in my opinion has led scholarship down a blind alley. The problematic of the identification will become clear in later chapters.

21. *Kingdom of God*, p. 167.

22. Ibid., p. 168; also: "The expression 'Kingdom of God' is in fact surprisingly rare in apocalyptic literature" (*Rediscovering*, p. 59, n. 1).

23. *Kingdom of God*, pp. 170–78. The texts are Mark 1:15; Luke 10:9–11; Matt. 10:7; Matt. 12:28; Luke 11:20; Matt. 11:12; Luke 17:20–21.

24. Ibid., pp. 174–78; *Rediscovering*, pp. 68–74; *Jesus and the Language*, pp. 43–45.

25. *Kingdom of God*, p. 178. In his final summary, pp. 184–85, Perrin seeks to minimize the implication for the apocalyptic character of Jesus' teaching.

26. *Rediscovering*, pp. 59–60.

27. Ibid., p. 60.

28. Ibid.

29. Specifically, in a detailed exegesis, Perrin rejects as authentic all of the so-called future Son of Man sayings.

30. *Rediscovering*, p. 31.

31. *Jesus and the Language*, p. 15.

32. Ibid., p. 29. Again on p. 32 the *Kaddish* reminds Perrin that the apocalyptic understanding was "never necessary nor universal."

33. Ibid., p. 40.

34. Cf. esp. ibid., p. 33. In this change Perrin is highly dependent upon the theoretical formulations of Philip Wheelwright and Paul Ricoeur. Ricoeur is among those to whom the book is dedicated.

35. Ibid., p. 29. The definition is taken from Philip Wheelwright, *Metaphor and Reality* (Bloomington: Indiana University Press, 1962, Midland Book Edition, 1968), p. 130. In our final chapter we will return to symbol for a fuller discussion.

36. Perrin proposes that Ricoeur's distinction between sign and symbol is similar to Wheelwright's steno- and tensive symbols, ibid., p. 30.

37. To use structuralist terminology, one will seek not ideational meaning but the meaning effect.

38. Ibid., p. 32.

39. The important essay of Günter Klein, "The Biblical Understanding of 'The Kingdom of God,'" surveys much the same material as Perrin and correctly concludes, "Within Judaism of Jesus' day, then, belief in God's rule existed in various forms" (*Interpretation* 26 [1972], p. 399). For Klein, within apocalypticism Kingdom is a peripheral phenomenon. The studies of both Perrin and Klein show that only a general understanding of the term can be derived from a diachronic analysis.

40. Reimarus seized this point at the beginning of historical criticism, and therefore it is appropriate that his insight become a starting point.

41. Even though only three parables have it as an expressed referent, Dodd, *The Parables of the Kingdom*, recognized the importance

of seeing the parables as related to Kingdom as metaphor to referent. Perrin, *Jesus and the Language*, p. 39, argues that all the parables "clearly have as their ultimate referent the Kingdom of God."

42. The distinction between diachronic and synchronic will be used throughout this book. Diachronic means literally through time and is roughly equivalent to historical. Synchronic means literally with time and is equivalent to contemporary. The distinction is borrowed from linguistics, where it is used to distinguish between a word's development in time and its actual functioning in a given speech act.

43. Dodd, *Parables of the Kingdom*, p. 5.

44. Perrin, *Jesus and the Language*, chap. 3, presents an extensive and critical discussion of recent parable criticism.

45. *LHWG*, pp. 133–62. John Dominic Crossan's *In Parables* (New York: Harper and Row, 1973), chapter 1 is a direct descendant of Funk's pioneering discussion.

46. *LHWG*, p. 136.

47. Ibid.

48. Ibid., p. 138.

49. Crossan has developed this point.

50. *LHWG*, p. 141.

51. Paul Ricoeur, "Biblical Hermeneutics," *Semeia* 4 (1975): 33–34.

52. *LHWG*, p. 53.

53. Given the similar functioning of both metaphor and symbol the equation in the case of parables is the following: A is to B as B is to C. C is the parable, B the symbol of the Kingdom of God, and A the suppressed referent of the symbol.

54. Funk, *LHWG*, p. 137, and Crossan, *In Parables*, p. 12, both make use of Lewis's distinction. (See note 55 below.)

55. C. S. Lewis, "Bluspels and Flalansferes," in *The Importance of Language*, ed. M. Black (Ithaca: Cornell University Press, 1969), pp. 30–56. The master's metaphor is what Funk describes as a simile. Neither Funk nor Lewis is bound by the grammatical distinction between metaphor and simile. For Funk (as for Lewis) a grammatical simile may in fact be a metaphor.

56. The pupil's metaphor is what Funk identifies as metaphor proper.

57. *In Parables*, p. 13.

58. Franz Kafka, *Parables and Paradoxes* (New York: Schocken Books, 1961), p. 11.

59. Funk, *LHWG*, p. 135, develops this point.

60. Crossan, *In Parables*, pp. 17–22, has forged a strong link

between poetic experience/poetic metaphor and the parallel religious experience/parable. "There is an intrinsic [*sic*] and inalienable bond between Jesus' experience and Jesus' parables. A sensitivity to the metaphorical language of religious and poetic experience and an empathy with the profound and mysterious linkage of such experience and such expression may help us to understand what is most important about Jesus: his experience of God" (p. 22).

61. "The American Home-World: Reality and Imagination." Lecture delivered in a series "Imagination and Contemporary Sensibility." University of Montana: quoted in Robert W. Funk, *Jesus as Precursor*, Semeia Studies (Philadelphia: Fortress Press and Missoula: Scholars Press, 1975), p. 66.

62. Ibid., p. 67. For the remainder of this book, when capitalized, World will have this technical sense.

63. *Method in Theology* (New York: Herder and Herder, 1972), p. 213.

64. Ibid., p. 10.

65. Ibid., p. 213.

66. Ibid.

2

NARRATIVE PARABLES

The English word "parable"[1] is a transliteration of the Greek *parabolē*, which renders the Hebrew *mashal*. As a literary classification, *mashal* denotes a variety of genres.[2] It can refer to extended metaphors, example stories, the visions of apocalyptic seers, or allegories. This diversity of type creates problems of definition.

At the beginning of modern parable research, Adolf Jülicher made a number of distinctions restricting the classification "parable." Initially, he distinguished between allegory and parable. For Jülicher allegory was an esoteric, mysterious story whose meaning or key lay outside, while parable was a simple, open story whose meaning was contained within.[3] But he further distinguished between *Gleichnisse* (similitudes), *Parabeln* (parables), and *Beispielerzählungen* (example stories).[4] Parable differed from similitude in the method of comparison: similitude compared two items while the parable developed a figurative story. Similitude dealt with a typical event or condition, whereas parable seized upon a particular situation. But as later critics admitted, this distinction is difficult to maintain in practice.[5] Example story is similar to parable in that it is a story, but it lacks a figurative element.

Jülicher's distinctions have remained current, but the quest for a definition of parabolic form in recent years has raised serious questions about the categories. An inherent difficulty is that the Semitic term *mashal* is simply too generic to be of much help. As a category of discrimination it is too broad. Jülicher's instinct toward a finer discrimination was correct, but his distinctions were inadequate because the distinction between

parable and example story is dependent upon subjective interpretation.[6] Finally, recent discussion of metaphor (see above) has
blurred distinctions between similitude and parable. The theory
of metaphor has served as an informal definition of parable.[7]

In this study we will distinguish between narrative and one-
line parables.[8] Both groups of parables are metaphors. Narrative
parables have plot, motion, characterization—they are mini
short stories. One-line parables are aphoristic, their language
dense, compact, jarring. Thus their semantic construction determines the classification.

Critical analysis of Jesus' parables faces several problems
which limit the interpretative range. Because of conditions
under which the material was transmitted,[9] parables cannot be
arranged in a chronological order. This eliminates any observation concerning development of themes in the corpus of parables.[10]

Likewise, problems of reconstruction are such that frequently
the text to be exegeted is highly controversial. The reconstructive
task cannot be avoided, but because in my judgment the reconstruction of certain parables was too difficult to produce a high
degree of probability, they have been left out of consideration.[11]

Finally, a relation between Jesus' biography and parables is
impossible to ascertain, since we possess no reliable outline of
his life.[12] This problem is complicated even further because the
gospel context is frequently either the creation of an evangelist
or the oral tradition. For a critical interpretation, the parable
itself must provide adequate clues. This is not an abandonment
of historical method, for the general context of interpretation
still remains first-century Palestine, but it does mean that the
precise historical context is no longer available (if it ever was
available).[13]

In this chapter we will analyze four narrative parables in the
following fashion. First, the setting within the Gospel(s) will be
discussed. It is often necessary to isolate the parable so as to
determine the redactional intention. Where necessary we will
attempt to reconstruct the parable. The main part of the analysis
will then follow. Our method will be to "read" the text. This
will involve first exposing the parable's underlying narrative

structure with the aim of making clear the narrative's plot and metaphorical motion. But at the same time, this structure affects a hearer from whose viewpoint a parable is semantic potential. A reading is a performance that actualizes that potential. We are concerned to describe a hearer's performance.

Finally, following the narrative analysis, we will develop a series of five theses to describe the phenomenal World which has generated this particular linguistic expression of that World.

JERUSALEM TO JERICHO
(Luke 10:30–35)

It may strike some as strange to select this narrative for our first parable,[14] for Bultmann clearly expresses the general scholarly consensus when he classifies this story not as parable proper, but example story.[15] The title "Good Samaritan" indicates the tradition's concurrence. But despite this handicap, the parable is appropriate, since if it can be shown to be a parable and not an example story, what is meant by parable will be all the clearer, because a new insight will have been forged in the reader's vision.

The Lucan context has controlled the perception of this story. Jeremias, maintaining Luke 10:25–29 as part of the original setting, claims that the lawyer's own answer to his first question about what he should do to inherit eternal life demands the problematic of "Who is my neighbor?"[16] Thus the Good Samaritan's story serves to provide an example, albeit a radical one, of who a good neighbor is.

But the interpretation runs aground for several reasons. From a form critical perspective it is false to assume that the evangelical context belongs to the original strata of a story. A comparison with Mark 12:28–34 and Matt. 22:34–40 shows that the lawyer's question is found in both Mark and Q. The parable's absence from Matthew indicates it was probably not in Q, and likewise its omission in Mark shows that the lawyer's question and the parable are not inseparably bound. Originally then Luke 10:25–28 circulated independently of the parable. "Neighbor" is also used in two different senses in this section of Luke. In vv. 27, 29, and 36, neighbor is the one to whom something is done, that is, "Whom must I love?" while in the parable neighbor is one who does something to me.[17] This difference is confirmed by Robert Funk's observation: "In the traditional reading of the parable the significance of the Samaritan has been completely effaced: the Samaritan is not a mortal enemy, but a good fellow, the model of virtuous deportment. Further, the auditors were no longer Jews but *goyim* (i.e., non-Jews)."[18] For these reasons one must reject the Lucan context as the focus which demands the story be viewed as an example of a good neighbor.

Funk's observation concerning the "Good" Samaritan being the creation of *goyim* auditors raises the important methodological question of point of view. Since we are seeking a unified insight, what perspective is appropriate for such an insight? Methodologically, the appropriate point of view is the auditor's, for parable itself stands between us and teller. By means of the historical imagination we will reconstruct the point of view of the audience to whom the parable was addressed: first-century Palestinian Jews. The viewpoint of first-century Judaism is a general referential nexus,[19] conflict with and resonance within which provide the occasion of meaning, the meaning effect. Exegesis' function is to provide the opportunity for hearing anew.

To facilitate development of point of view I have adopted a structuralist methodology. Each parable text has been divided into a series of lexies, i.e., single units that provide a basis for analysis. These units' limits are arbitrary, and their significance is simply that they are small units of narrative action. This procedure enables us to keep the text firmly in front of us during the discussion. I have also adopted the structuralist "contract" model as a means of analyzing the plot motion.[20]

Lexie 1.   Initial Action (v. 30)

The audience sees a man making a journey from Jerusalem to Jericho, a distance of about seventeen miles. The man on a journey is the only consistent character in the story. The road between Jerusalem and Jericho was well-known to be dangerous.[21] He is attacked by robbers, beaten, and left for half-dead. His journey interrupted, he is left passive in the ditch. The man, now in the ditch, has been installed as subject.[22] While the audience sympathizes with him, since an everyday situation has been noted, they are not forced to identify with him because in a story that begins with a tragedy helpers are sure to come along. An audience will prefer to identify with a helper/hero.[23]

Many questions, raised by this first lexie, go unanswered because they do not bear on the story. Why, for example, was the man making a trip? Why was he alone on a dangerous road? To raise such questions is natural, but they will remain unanswered.

Lexie 2.   Two Possibilities (vv. 31–32)

A possible helper/hero immediately appears on the scene, a priest. He is an acceptable figure with which to identify, except that he does not offer help but passes by on the other side. Likewise with the Levite, the next figure. These two reinforce each other and serve the same function: they offer and then take away possible identifications on the audience's part. Meanwhile the man remains in the ditch. While the audience has no objection to identifying with priest and Levite, their refusal to help is not fatal for the audience, since as Jeremias points out, the callous attitude of the priest and Levite easily feed upon anticlerical suspicions.[24] The audience now expects a Jewish layman to come to the rescue.

Lexie 3.   Denouement (vv. 33–35)

The next character is not the expected Jewish layman but a Samaritan, the Jew's mortal enemy. Nor does he cooperate with the audience by passing on, but has compassion. The audience now faces a cruel dilemma: identify with the Samaritan or get into the ditch. The first they cannot do; the second is distasteful. But into the ditch they must go. Once in the ditch the victim does not consent to the Samaritan's ministrations; he must submit. The Samaritan binds his wounds and takes him to an inn. The innkeeper is given two denarii, which is enough to provide boarding for about twenty-four days.[25] The Samaritan will return, and the man in the ditch will continue to be obligated to him.

The descriptions of the various characters call for specific responses from the audience. There is a man, as unspecified he has the widest, most plastic appeal; bandits, negative figures;[26] priest and Levite, who in turn represent positive and negative responses; and finally the Samaritan, who provokes in the audience a totally negative response. The value characterization ultimately forces the audience to identify with the man in the ditch.

Likewise the construction of the surface Greek text supports such an identification. The scenes of the priest and Levite as well as the Samaritan's opening part are closely parallel.

A (1) By chance a certain priest
    (2) was going down on that road
        (3) and seeing him
            (4) he passed by.

B (1) Likewise a Levite
    (2) upon that place coming
        (3) and seeing
            (4) he passed by.

C (1) A Samaritan
    (2) traveling
        came upon him
        (3) and seeing
            (4) he had compassion.

The opening phrases of A and B ("By chance," "Likewise") point up the fortuitous circumstances of the events and place the two scenes in conjunction. By contrast C(1) is stark: "A Samaritan." This accentuates the negative value asssociated with this character.

A(2) and B(2) are again set in chiasmic parallelism: verb/prepositional phrase; prepositional phrase/verb. C(2) is made up of two phrases recalling A(2) and B(2). In the Greek *hodeuōn* ("traveling") recalls *hodō* (road) of A(2); B(2) is chiasmic to C(2): B(2) "upon that place coming"/C(2) "came upon him." C(2) marks a shift in that A(2) and B(2) place the priest and Levite in the vicinity of the victim, while C(2) draws the Samaritan and the victim into personal relation. From the audience's vantage I would suggest that the phrase "came upon him" is viewed as a threat.

A(3), B(3), and C(3) ("seeing") are the same in all three sequences. They function to draw the characters together so that a decision can be made.

Finally, the verb that ends each scene provides the real power of the audience's identification. The Samaritan's compassion contrasts sharply with the priest and Levite "passing by." Furthermore C's construction delays the Samaritan's response. He is introduced immediately in C(1), whereas priest and Levite are mentioned only in the end of A(1) and B(1) respectively. C(2) is longer than A(2) or B(2). Thus there is a greater distance between his mention in C(1) and the description of his action in C(4). This is further emphasized by the elaborate description of his dealing with the victim. C's careful construction teases the audience before its fateful decision is demanded.

The parable can be summarized as follows: to enter Kingdom one must get into the ditch and be served by one's mortal enemy. Of course, to summarize the parable in this manner is already to risk a loss of meaning. That is, to truly understand one must enter the parable so that its contours can resonate. The parable is an invitation to enter, but in order to enter one must in a sense undergo a conversion, in which the parable becomes a lens refracting everyday experience under the symbol Kingdom of God.[27]

In chapter 1 we argued that the metaphorical character of the parable represents the referential nexus of Jesus' World. To put it another way, parables work out in language Jesus' experience of Kingdom. To enter the parable's World is to discover a new horizon of meaning that orientates a hearer to the experience of Kingdom. Since parables are generated by the referential nexus of Jesus, his World, and are meant to provide experience of that referential nexus, it should be possible to spell out or delineate that horizon. To do this I am proposing five theses, outlined below. These accentuate common themes in parables, and in turn each parable will add depth and precision to the theses. In chapter 4 the theses will provide a descriptive foundation, derived from the study of individual parables, by which to construct a formal model of Jesus' World.

The theses are not attempts to reduce the parable to discursive propositions or to even say what a parable means, but attempts to suggest in outline the dimensions of the horizon of Jesus' World. They aim, by means of a metalanguage (language about language), to consolidate insight into parables. Finally, by way of caveat, I would not claim that the theses are exhaustive or exclusive; others could and probably should have been developed. But these appeared to me to form a consistent horizon of parable.

Thesis I.   The comic appears under the guise of tragedy

Comedy and tragedy are technical terms derived ultimately from Aristotle. A comic plot is one in which the protagonist moves toward well-being, while in a tragic plot he moves toward downfall.[28] By extension the terms can describe visions of reality, how one approaches and organizes experience. In a strict literary sense our first parable's plot is comic, since a protagonist, the man in the ditch, is rescued and his well-being assured in the final verse. As a window into Jesus' World the parable in this case shows that World to be ultimately comic. But this is comedy wherein the path of the protagonist moves toward tragedy. By falling into the ditch he immediately faces tragedy. He does not risk tragedy; he is forced into the ditch. Comedy appears under tragedy's guise when the audience must decide between identifying with the Samaritan or getting into the ditch. The audience has a third option: to withdraw from the World of parable. To achieve a comic ending, whoever enters the parable must be able to risk increasing tragedy, under the guise of submitting to the Samaritan.

Thesis II.   Grace comes to those who have no other alternative

This traditional theological terminology reformulates the first thesis in a different context. There is no indication that the man in the ditch was particularly happy to have the Samaritan come

to his rescue. In fact, he may well have preferred to take his
chances with a Jewish layman and to have remained in the ditch.
Grace comes to those who cannot resist, who have no other
alternative than to accept it. To enter the parable's World, to
get into the ditch, is to be so low that grace is the only alternative. The point may be so simple as this: only he who needs
grace can receive grace.

Thesis III.   In the World of the parable the secular and religious are congruous

This is deduced from two aspects of parable. Because it is not
allegory, does not have some predetermined referent outside,[29] the
parable turns a hearer back to everyday experience as paradigm
for religious experience. Secondly, entrance into the parable
prevents the equation of the parable's individual figures with
religious symbols. The whole parable becomes a lens through
which one is invited to view oneself and surroundings. This
"everydayness," rearranged by parable, becomes the way by
which one approaches Kingdom. To escape parable is to forfeit
the possibility of that reality. To convert parable into a substitute for a known religious symbol is to refuse to face parable as
parable. It does violence to parable's claim that the fragments of
our everydayness are reconstructed into the World of the parable.

Thesis IV.   The World of the hearer is questioned by the World of parable

"World" is used in this thesis for referential nexus, or horizon of
meaning, as discussed above. A parable's everydayness does not
mean that it simply points back to everyday experience. The
parabolic World's strangeness suggests that everydayness has
been rearranged. Parable makes a burlesque of everyday order.
A hearer's vision focuses so that one's World, i.e., the context
that grants meaning, is called into question. "Jew" not only
must accept Samaritan as helper (savior) but is obliged to enter
the ditch to be saved. This involves a twofold response. The
hearer enters the parable's World and then, reflecting back,
acknowledges that this is the Kingdom of God.

**Thesis V.   Faith appears here as the ability to trust
the depiction of World in the parable**

Faith is the hearer's response as he enters the parable's strange
new World. It is required by parable itself, but also, implicitly,
one has faith in the parable teller, in his ability to perceive and
reorganize reality. Finally, there is the teller's faith in his own
vision. If one climbs into the ditch, what guarantee is there that
the Samaritan will help rather than murder? Can one trust the
parable teller to provide a comic ending in a tragic situation?
Can the parable teller trust his parable not to betray the one he
has invited in?

We will test the validity of these five theses for the remaining
parables. Our method will remain the same: after a reading of
each parable, the theses will be examined so as to give them
greater specificity. The reading of each parable must organize
the theses or else the parable will lose its primacy.

A GREAT BANQUET
(Matthew 22:1–14; Luke 14:15–24; Gospel of Thomas 64)

In Jerusalem to Jericho the critical effort necessary to recover
the parable's original stratum was relatively easy. We had to
denote the limits of the parable and then to disengage it from
the Lucan context. With the present parable the critical problems are considerably more complicated. While the parable's
three extant versions exhibit considerable variation, the general
consensus supposes a common parable as source of this diverse
tradition.[30]

For some problems, solutions are obvious. In Luke and
Thomas a man holds a feast and a single servant handles the
invitations, while in Matthew a *king* gives a *marriage* feast and
servants deliver invitations. Matthew has servants, since it is
more fitting for a king to have servants rather than a servant.[31]
Likewise, king and marriage feast are secondary additions. As
Bultmann suggests, the marriage feast has an allegorical ring
and Matthew's Greek betrays the development toward "king" by
referring to "man/king." Luke's and Thomas's agreement on the
more simple arrangement attests to their probable originality.

In the Matthean version servants issue two calls to the invited. In the first instance, the guests simply refuse, whereupon the king sends the servants again. Second time around the guest make light of the invitation. Two excuses are given, "while the rest seized his servants, treated them shamefully, and killed them" (v. 6). With this act, everydayness has broken down and the arrangement of a wedding feast is suddenly out of hand. The king sends his army to destroy their city and his servants out into the thoroughfares to gather "as many as you can find."

Jeremias has suggested that this section of the Matthean parable is an allegory illustrating salvation history.[32] Matthew has redacted Mark's outline by inserting two parables (Two Sons and Wedding Feast) to heighten the salvation history theme implicit in Mark. In the preceding parable, Wicked Husbandmen, Matthew consistently accentuated the narrative's allegorical tendency toward a history of salvation interpretation. For example, according to Jeremias, Matthew sees, in the sending of two servants as against Mark's one, references to the earlier and later prophets. This allegorical tendency is carried over into the parable of the Wedding Feast. The first sending of the servants refers to the prophets, the second to the apostles. For this reason, the explicit reference to the readiness of the feast is held off until after the first sending. Since there is no sending of the son as in the Wicked Husbandmen, in its place is the feast's announcement. The second servants (apostles) are killed (martyred), and the king sends his troops to destroy their city, which for Jeremias refers to the destruction of Jerusalem. A final sending of servants to those in the thoroughfares corresponds to the mission to the Gentiles.

Matthew's conclusion also differs from those of Luke and Thomas. For Matthew, servants go out and collect all whom they find, "both bad and good" (v. 10). After filling the hall, there follows the story of the guest with no wedding garment, who is cast out into the outer darkness. This is completely missing in Luke and Thomas and is an addition based upon Matthean theology. Günther Bornkamm has isolated the theme of coming judgment and the present mixed community, which is Matthew's way of relating ecclesiology and eschatology.[33] The parable's gathering of "both the good and the bad" reflects this mixed church, while the addendum of the wedding garment means that membership in the church is not sufficient—"by their fruits you will know them" (Matt. 7:16).

This survey of Matthew's redaction allows us to identify Matthean additions and shifts of emphasis. The following items are secondary accretions: king, marriage feast, servants (instead of servant), the first sending to the guests, the destruction of the city, very possibly the addition in v. 10 of the reference to "both bad and good," and the concluding story of the man without a wedding garment.

In contrast, the Lucan version is simpler and lacks many of Matthew's allegorical traits. The problematic element in Luke is the double invitation to the *un*invited (vv. 21–23). Jeremias argues that the second invitation (v. 23) expands the original parable to signal the Gentile's inclusion, a theme held in common with Matthew.[34] Robert Funk disputes this identification of the second invitation as the creation of Luke's theology of the Gentile mission, maintaining that such a reading is based upon transposing Matthew's ideology into Luke and that nothing in the Lucan story overtly points in this direction.[35]

A double invitation to the uninvited is a problem, both because it is missing in Matthew and Thomas and because of the high possibility that the second invitation is an allegorical reference to the Gentile mission. A critical grasp can be obtained by examining the Lucan context. The parable is part of the so-called travel narrative (9:51—19:27) and is set more immediately in the context of table talk at a Pharisee's house (14:1). It is preceded immediately by special Lucan material which concludes, "But when you give a feast, invite the poor, the maimed, the lame, the blind, and you will be blessed, because they cannot repay you. You will be repaid at the resurrection of the just" (14:13–14). For Luke, the parable functions as an example of this principle. Thus redactionally, the suspect verse is 21b (the first invitation) which repeats the command of vv. 13–14. Verse 22 likewise is suspect because it is a connecting link between 21b and 23.

Gospel of Thomas's version[36] formally agrees with the reconstructed form of Luke. The main difference concerns the servant's repeating the invitation before each guest gives his excuse.

This shifts emphasis to the excuses of the invited which is made clear in the conclusion: "Tradesmen and merchants shall not enter the places of my Father." Since a prominent theme in Thomas is the rejection of the tradesmen and merchants, it is natural to emphasize their excuses.

A final point is the variety of excuses given by the invited. The following scheme shows both similarities and divergencies.

MATTHEW	LUKE	THOMAS
Goes to a farm	Bought a farm	Bought a house
		Bought a village
Business		Claims against a merchant
	Bought five yoke of oxen	
	Married a wife	A friend to be marrried

There appears to be no way to determine the original excuses and, if the parable was told more than once, there may have been several different excuses. But at least two of the excuses probably have a high claim: some excuse involving a farm and somebody either getting married or helping a friend who is getting married. Very likely three excuses are part of the form.[37]

We can now turn our attention to a reading of the parable.

Lexie 1.   Situation (Luke 14:16b)

The audience is offered a picture of a man who has prepared a great banquet to which he has invited many. He is apparently wealthy if he can afford to give a banquet for many. The occasion is left unspecified, as well as the social status of those invited, although like the host they are probably wealthy.

Lexie 2.   Sending of the Servant (v. 17)

The audience now recognizes that the invited are among the socially elite, for the repetition of the invitation at the time of the banquet was a special courtesy practiced by the upper classes.[38] The banquet is now ready, all is waiting for the party to start.

Lexie 3.   Refusal (vv. 18–20)

The invited's universal refusal is puzzling and strains the parable's everydayness. The social status of the invited is confirmed by their very excuses. We are dealing with landowners. Jeremias calculates that a man who buys five yoke of oxen owns at least forty-five hectares, considerably more than the average peasant.[39] But the excuses themselves are not important, for they stand as examples and are not meant to be the exclusive reasons for refusal. If many were invited, this certainly means more than three. The point is that "they all alike began to make excuses." But why excuses now? They had previously accepted the invitation and the servant was only performing the courtesy invitation. Their action appears in concert. Why do they *all* refuse to come? Is this a case of social snobbery? The parable gives no answer— the audience is left only with their refusal.

Lexie 4.   Report to Master (v. 21a)

The master's plan has aborted, and with that the story itself is threatened. The would-be host has three options. He may call off the feast, thus wasting the food since the feast is ready. He may punish those who have refused to honor his invitation. Matthew's version, taking the option literally, has a king destroy their city. The man in the original version has no such drastic recourse. The most he could do would be to exclude them from his company in the future.[40] Either of these first two options abort his great feast. If his plan is to succeed, then he faces an emergency, for he cannot wait too long or else the food will spoil.

Lexie 5.   Action (v. 23)[41]

Faced with emergency, he acts in a decisive fashion, sending his servant out to gather the riffraff to fill up his hall. As Jeremias points out, to "compel the people to come in" reflects that in the East the poor, as a matter of courtesy and modesty, would resist "the invitation to the entertainment until they are taken by the hand and gently forced to enter the house."[42] So even the

poor do not rush in at the chance for a fine party. In taking his
decisive action, the householder goes from one extreme to the
other: from the social elite to the bottom of the social scale,
skipping the large number in between. But they are of no concern. Everything is sketched in either/ors: all the elite refuse,
only the poorest are invited. Finally, as though to accentuate
this either/or policy, the householder demands that the banquet
hall be filled. Why this is so important is not specified, although
the audience could guess—to prevent those originally invited
from changing their minds.

The parable presents the auditors with several possible identifications. In the first parable we considered, the audience had to
choose between identification with Samaritan or man in the
ditch. In this parable it is different. Structurally, the subject is
the man who gives a feast; he issues the mandate and attempts
to fulfill that mandate. The servant acts as his surrogate. For
example, when those invited make their excuses, they really are
not speaking to the servant, but to the host through the servant.
The servant is a vehicle to facilitate the story's movement. The
man or his surrogate is the only figure who appears in every
scene, so he is constituted as subject. The tradition has insisted,
as with many parables, upon seeing the subject elsewhere. As
we have seen, the allegory has two subjects, the first invited and
then the second invited. Identification with the host has been
blocked, for allegorically he stands for God.

The auditors face a choice. They can identify with the subject of the story, the householder, or perhaps in turn with the
two groups of invited. The audience's options work out in the
following manner: if identification occurs with those originally
invited, it effectively leads nowhere when they refuse; but if the
hearer still wants to come to the feast (and to enter the parable's
World one must go to the feast), then he must come on the new
terms now set by the host. The parable's movement is similar to
that of the Samaritan: to come to the feast one must dwell in
the highways and hedges. Only with such will the banquet hall
be filled. Such an identification is possible and is one element
of a complex identification process at work within the parable.

A primary identification is with the host, for everyone, poor and rich alike, dreams of giving the great feast to impress friends. All is ready for the party; the invitations have been sent in advance, the food is prepared, and the servant goes to bring those invited. But tragedy strikes: every guest refuses to come, and no matter what the excuse is good or bad, the party is still ruined. The man reacts immediately: he sends his servant to gather in the outcast. But why the outcast? And given the open ending of the parable, will they come? The audience faces a dilemma: they threw a party and nobody came; now they must invite nobodies to fill the room. The parable says to throw a grand ball you must invite nobodies. Not much of a choice to make.

The relation between this parable and our first one is close, and several theses underpinning that parable's World operate here. For example, in this parable the secular and religious are congruent (Thesis III). This is most evident when the allegorical interpretation is eliminated and the host is allowed his function as subject. Likewise, faith is the ability to trust the depiction of World in the parable (Thesis V). But these I take to be minor accents.

A major component of the parable's referential nexus is represented by Thesis I: The comic appears under the guise of tragedy. There are moments of pain and humor, for instead of the sedate feast of the elite the man ends with a mob of the socially outrageous. The sight of beggars being escorted into the hall presents a somewhat amusing picture. The same is true of everyone making excuses and fleeing the feast. There is here a burlesque of a banquet.[43] One would almost suppose that the Marx brothers were the caterers!

The burlesque element is for the audience's entertainment, and was surely lost on the victim of this social event of the year. The story begins with a comic possibility of a banquet, and since all is prepared, little stands in the way of a comic ending. After all, what can go wrong once the food is prepared? If for some unexpected reason a guest or two might excuse themselves, it would pose no serious problems. But the unthinkable happens: the feast is threatened with tragedy, since every guest declines. What can the host do? He invites the outcast, that is, he offers gospel, good news. He thereby risks tragedy for a possibly comic outcome. The host very definitely takes a risk. He is risking his community standing by going outside his social group. He risks also that the outcast will turn down his invitation. Furthermore, the banquet achieved will be quite different from the one proposed. In relation to what he had set out, the final feast has the appearance of a rump session.[44] To hold a banquet, he must face the tragedy of no banquet, and if he persists in holding a banquet, it must be of a quite different character. To hold a banquet one must invite only the outcast; to go to a banquet one must be the outcast.

The parable calls into question the hearer's World (Thesis IV). Having set his plans, the host has calculated reality. His World is supposed to perform in a predictable way. But it fails; it rejects him. The man must proclaim gospel to the outcast if he is to discover a World in which to dwell. Here the parable's either/or motion comes into play. The host chooses which World he wants to enter. To hold his banquet he abandons his customary World and enters a World that must appear strange to one with a servant. The hearer, in the guise of the man, is called upon to examine the predictability of his World (will they come to the feast?), to decide that they will not, and then immediately to opt for another strange World whose only characteristic is that it is among the highways and hedges.

A challenge to predictability pertains to parable as metaphor for Kingdom. As a story, it could be a clever example of social snobbery. The host, rejected by the elite, in turn snubs them by inviting their opposite numbers. An element of social one-upmanship is part of the story's appeal. But the real challenge to the hearer's World is the conjunction of narrative and Kingdom. To argue that such is Kingdom is to destroy the Kingdom's very predictability. To realize that this is Yahweh's ruling activity is to dwell in a World gone riot.

GOING ON A JOURNEY
(Matthew 25:14–30; Luke 19:11–27)

This parable is important for our purposes because at first glance it seems to contradict or call for a reformulation of Thesis I, that the comic appears in the guise of tragedy. Dan Via maintains that this is an example of a tragic parable.[45] It is not necessarily true that a parable with a tragic plot would a priori call into question the relation between comic and tragedy in Jesus' worldview. But a parable that has been interpreted as tragedy will test and clarify the meaning of Thesis I.

Luke's parable normally is seen as a conflation of two separate stories, those of the Pounds and the Throne Claimant.[46] The Throne Claimant appears in 19:12b, 14–15a, 27. The servants' reward of cities derives from this theme. The man making the journey becomes a nobleman seeking a kingdom. As Jeremias points out, the fusion of the two stories is made very problematic at v. 24, where the giving of ten pounds to one who already has control over cities makes little sense.[47]

Matthew has cast the parable in the context of a discussion of the Parousia, so that the parable's master is the returning Lord.[48] Intrusions into the parable resulting from the story's adaptation to illustrate judgment at the Parousia can be seen in the speech to the faithful servants, "enter into the joy of your master" (25: 21b, 23b), and the faithless servant's condemnation in v. 30.[49] Verse 29 (19:26 in Luke) is a free-floating logion attached to the parable during its circulation in the oral tradition.[50]

The parable exhibits a careful symmetrical arrangement of three scenes.[51] Scene I depicts the situation (vv. 14–15): a man going on a journey entrusts his property to his servants. A threefold division of property is described and the man leaves. Scene II (vv. 16–18) shows the servants managing the master's money. Scene III begins in v. 19 with the master's return and the inevitable accounting. This scene is divided into three sequences, one for each servant. Two servants are judged good, the third bad.

Via remarks in his analysis that the answers of the five- and two-talent men "are essentially in the same form as that of the one-talent man."[52] On the surface this is quite true. But the subtle differences give valuable hints for interpretation. The five- and two-talent-men sequences are identical and reinforce each other. Double reinforcement is a common pattern in Jesus' parables. The priest/Levite performed such a function in "Jerusalem to Jericho." The first subsequence of Scene III can be schematized as follows.

Scene III, sequence 1:   ten-talent man

A. The master has issued a contract to the servants which is now due. (This is the general heading of the three episodes that follow. A is assumed in each sequence.)
B. The five-talent man comes forward bringing five more talents.
C. He reports to the master a profit of five talents.
D. The master compliments the servant.
E. He gives him more responsibility.

Significantly, the master does not receive back the ten talents, but only a report of what has happened.

Scene III, sequence 3:   one-talent man

A. (Assumed)
B. The servant comes forward.
C_1. He chastises the master with the accusation that he is a hard man, "reaping where you did not sow, and gathering where you did not winnow, . . ."
C. He reports on his activity.
C_2. He attempts to return the talent to his master ("Here you have what is yours").
D. The master chastises the servant.
D_1. He implies the servant's activity is inconsistent with his picture of the master.
E. He punishes the servant and gives the talent to the ten-talent man.

The difference between sequences 1 and 3 comes in C and D. In sequence 3, the one-talent servant comes forward, just as the other two servants had, to announce the completion of his contract. Meanwhile, the audience and servant are aware that he cannot complete his contract, because in Scene II the servant's burial of his talent does not bode well for the time of reckoning. The forewarning is important because of the servant's complaint that the master is an unjust and rapacious man.

Aware of his failure, the servant does not begin C with a

report as did the first two servants. Instead he attacks the master, as a hard man, "a rapacious man, heedlessly intent on his own profit," as Jeremias says.[53] The attack serves two purposes. It draws attention away from the servant's failure by blaming it on the master. Secondly, the servant appeals to the audience by conjuring up the typical picture of the oriental despot. With this stereotype ("This is how masters are") he draws them to his side. Only then does he report his action, that he buried the talent in the ground.

This report is parallel to that of the other two servants. In C_2 the servant gives the talent back to the master with the implication that he is fulfilling his contract. Actually, he is seeking to renegotiate the original contract by insisting that the talent's return is all the master is entitled to, even though his complaint against the master indicates the original contract calls for more than simple preservation. This is the first instance of the master receiving back talents he has given servants to invest.

In section D of sequence 1 the master blessed the servant for his good work. In D of sequence 3 he curses the servant. The functions are in opposition. But in D_1 the master answers the servant's attack upon his character by pointing out that the servant's activity was inconsistent with his picture of the master.[54] If he were such a harsh man, who reaps where he did not sow, why did the servant not at least deposit the money in a bank so that the master might collect his interest? D_1 argues that the servant's justification for his inactivity does not justify his position, but is inconsistent. A question mark is set against both the servant's rationalization of his behavior and his description of the master.

Verse 28 (function E) serves the same function in this sequence as did E in sequence 1: the judgment's implications are carried out. The talent is taken away from the third servant and given to the first. The master does not accept the servant's offer (C_2) to take the talent back, but gives it instead to the ten-talent man. The master has not taken back any talents he gave to the first two servants, but has increased their holdings. To give the talent to the first servant draws attention back to the way he dealt with that servant.

In the two parables previously discussed, the subject was the character who appeared in every scene. There is no such figure in this parable, since servants come on and off stage, while the master is missing in Scene II. But the master's coming and going unifies the story, providing possibilities for action. From a structural perspective the master is the parable's subject. But if the master is the subject, he nevertheless has competition from the third servant.[55]

With these preliminary observations in mind, we turn to examine the parable's narrative structure.

Lexie 1.   Preparation for Journey (Matthew 25:14–15)

The story begins in an innocent enough fashion. A man is going on a journey, and being a man of wealth he entrusts his property to servants. It is certainly presupposed that the property is to be increased during his absence.[56] The audience's response to this first lexie is simple observation. While the man is the clear subject of the lexie, he does designate the servants as subject of the following sequences.

Lexie 2.   The Servants (vv. 16–18)

The audience views the servants' activity while the master is gone. Two servants double what has been entrusted to them, while the third simply preserves it. This lexie is a summary scene, since only the outcomes of the servants' actions are important. The audience is given no details. As pointed out above, the audience now is forewarned that by comparison the fate of the third servant does not bode well.

Lexie 3.   First Two Servants' Accounting (vv. 19–23)

The master's return provides the narrative possibility for the final scene. I have divided it into two lexies because sequences 1 and 2 function differently from sequence 3. This lexie consists of two identical sequences. Since the master's character is impugned in sequence 3, what picture of the master and his relationship with the first two servants emerges in this lexie? What impression will the audience draw? The picture is neutral. The servants are not fearful, but confident in what they have accomplished. Likewise the master is not pictured as judge (despite the fact that an accounting is taking place) but as recipient of a report. Furthermore, in his response to the servants the master does not act as though what they have done is expected simply as a matter of course, but is lavish in his praise and entrusts them with increased responsibility. He does not demand the talents back from the servants. By the lexie's conclusion the audience has no indication that the master is a tyrant, rather quite the opposite, that he is generous. The proceedings have been amicable.

Lexie 4.   Third Servant's Accounting (vv. 24–25)

Before reporting what has happened, the servant attacks the master's character. His picture of the master, derived from a stereotype of an oriental despot, draws the audience to his support. As we have seen, the master's image to this point is at least neutral, but most certainly he has not behaved as a despot. The third servant's charge forces the audience to choose between the master's stereotype and his actions. The servant, remarking that he was afraid, reports that he buried his talent in the ground. He attempts to return the talent, which is a subtle claim to the audience that his contract has been fulfilled. Once again the stereotype image of master comes into play. If the audience believes the servant's charge, his offer to return the talent implies he is a victim of the despot. Should the master punish him, he will be living up to the social stereotype.

Lexie 5.   Master's Response (vv. 26–28)

The master's initial response seems to vindicate the stereotype of despot: "You wicked and slothful servant!" Viewed as a despot, the curse is both expected and unjust; expected because he is a hard man and unjust because he should have been satisfied with not losing his talent. He continues with a question: If you knew I was such, why did you not take appropriate action? His question both indicates that the servant himself does not believe his own characterization, and challenges the audience to revise its stereotyped view. When the talent is taken from the servant, the one who views the master as despot judges this rank injustice.[57] But this is not so since the servant has already offered the return of the talent. The free giving of the talent to the one who has ten talents harks back to the master's dealing with the first servant. The talent is not kept for the master but given to the first servant. The audience sees injustice compounded. But if the stereotyped view is rejected, then the parable reveals generosity. The audience has to decide which perspective to take. If it persists in its stereotyped view of the master as despot, it cannot enter parable; if it rejects that image and looks at things as they are, it can enter the parable.

The parable questions the World of the hearer by the juxtaposition of the parabolic World (Thesis IV). In A Great Banquet the everyday World's predictability was challenged within the parable when plans for the feast went astray. Here a direct appeal is made outside the parable to the hearer. The stereotyped prejudice against masters is represented by the third servant. Tension between stereotype and reality is created when the master questions the servant's characterization of him by pointing back to his own activity with the first two servants. Ultimately the parable asks, "How does one judge, or how does one construct a World?" At first glance the two questions seem different, but they are identical. One judges on the basis of criteria; World as referential nexus is one's criteria. If one uses for criterion the servant's stereotype of the master, then he will be judged cruel and hard; if the criteria are his actions, he will be seen as not only just, but also generous.

How do we live in a World? In accepting unchallenged the World into which we are thrown, we become its victim, just as the third servant is a victim of his own perceptions. If we are to break out of the World into which we are thrown, then we need to shift criteria, to shift horizon, to repent. When judgment conforms to a preconceived image, World is ideology. But in the parable the hearer must ask, "What really happened?" Then World is freedom, in that one can receive World as gift, as freely given. In an ideological World, we act under the ideology's compulsion. Nothing can be received, for everything is predetermined. But a free World is created by its own reception. A dweller in that World is free from the compulsion of judgment by ideology. But how do we become open to the experience of reality as it is, to receive its grace? No longer must we react in a predetermined fashion, but now as the situation demands. To enter the parable's World, to abandon the servant's stereotype, is to enter a new World where masters will be generous despite what one has been told. pretty good —

This notion is in turn related to Thesis II, that grace may be the last alternative. The third servant was unable to acknowledge his master as gracious because his image of the master would not allow it. He was afraid and therefore paralyzed. To receive grace he would have had to destroy his stereotyped view of the master before he had such evidence, i.e., before the first two servants' accounting. He did not accept grace because he did not see that he had no other alternative. Grace would have meant that he would have to take responsibility for his own action and would not have had the social stereotype to protect him.

This parable deals, at least on the surface level, with a social prejudice. It is a peasant's prejudice against the rich that provides metaphorical tension in the parable. Is this then a parable against social prejudice? No, for that would be to convert it into an allegory. Rather the parable takes a secular example (Thesis III), how servants relate to a master, and says this is how it is with the Kingdom. To enter the Kingdom one must abandon World, stereotype, and accept Kingdom as it is. It cannot be predetermined but gives itself as it is.[58]

Demand for faith is likewise explicit in this parable (Thesis V). To accept the parable, the hearer's faith must shift from the servant's stereotype to the master's actions. Such a shift occurs not because of the master's explicit repudiation of the servant's characterization but because of his actions. The hearer must be willing to trust the master's actions. After entering the parable, he must be willing to risk that the master will not betray him and revert to a despot. It is a very risky matter to enter the parable, for perhaps a villain lurks behind the master's guise; maybe the third servant is correct?

Our discussion of the parable began by taking notice of Dan Via's classification of the parable as tragic. "The tragic shape of the plot of the parable derives from the experience of the one-talent man."[59] The focal point for Via is the one-talent man. Via is at least partially correct. The one-talent man's end is only apparent tragedy, for at the conclusion he is still in the same state as in the beginning: he has no talent. On the other hand, within the parable master and third servant vie to determine the parable's shape. The hearer decides whether or not the parable is tragic. It is tragic only if one accepts the servant's accusation against the master.

If Via is correct only to a limited degree, does the parable have a comic ending? The comic appears in the guise of tragedy (Thesis I) only if one takes into consideration the active part the audience plays in the parable. For example, if the first two servants shared the third servant's image of the master, then they risked tragedy to achieve a comic ending. But there is no evidence that they shared the third servant's opinion. The audience, however, is asked to accept a comic outcome in a possibly tragic confrontation with the master. Because of their stereotype of the master, he poses the possibility of tragedy. To avoid tragedy they must accept the master as offering a comic possibility. If the parabolic World offers freedom, it is a freedom that means the abandonment of the predictability of the everyday.

A MAN HAD TWO SONS
(Luke 15:11–32)

The common title, "Parable of the Prodigal Son," is one that Luke would have accepted. Chapter 15 is a collection of parables whose theme is summarized in 15:2, "And the Pharisees and the scribes murmured, saying, 'This man receives sinners and eats with them.'" Parables of Lost Sheep, Lost Coin, and Prodigal Son provide examples of Kingdom coming to sinners who repent, not righteous Pharisees. The Lucan context[60] has led to two problems in the history of interpretation: (1) it demands an allegorization of the characters, and (2) it has forced the parable's accent to fall on the first part.

Jeremias's interpretation exemplifies the problems associated with a historical allegorization. The father is like God[61] and the younger son corresponds to the poor to whom the gospel is offered. Thus for Jeremias the accent falls upon the first part of the parable,[62] wherein the loving forgiveness of the father is demonstrated.

If the accent falls upon the first part, why is there a scene with an elder brother? "There can be only one answer, because of the actual situation. The parable was addressed to men who were like the elder brother, men who were offended at the gospel."[63] Pharisees are identified as the opponents by the redactional introduction at 15:2. While the parable is a vindication of Jesus' ministry, it remains open-ended for Jeremias, since Jesus does not pronounce judgment on them, hoping they will see how their self-righteousness separates them from God.[64]

But the openness creates an acute problem. If the parable challenges Pharisees to accept the gospel, as Jeremias maintains, why should they respond if according to 15:31 they are the only inheritors ("All that is mine is yours")?[65] If the parable describes what God is like, then he who is apparently generous in forgiving the younger son is playing a cruel joke on him. The elder son inherits all, so he can come into the feast and rejoice at his brother's return, for the younger is now the elder's slave.

If the Lucan context fails to interpret, we must turn, as with other parables, to the parable itself in search of internal clues for interpretation.

Lexie 1.   Request (vv. 11–12a)

The audience is presented a man with two sons. The opening verse's importance is often overlooked because it is so simple,[66] but in the narrative parables so far examined, the opening verses have presented the situation from which the audience will hear. In this parable the identifications of the sons are quite specific. The man has two sons (*duō hyious*); and immediately the younger son (*neōteros*) approaches his father for his share of the inheritance. The mention of a younger son alerts the hearer to the elder brother's existence. At some point the elder will make his appearance. Another parable dealing with a father and two sons occurs at Matt. 21:28–32. But there the sons are designated as *tekna* (literally children) and are only distinguished as *prōtos* (first) and *deuteros* (second). In Matthew the question of the sons' relative ages plays no part.

The detail of a younger son and the implied elder son is not simply added color, but an important detail, part of the parable's economy, that is, associated in the audience's mind with a particular set of traditional stories.

Stories about two sons play an important part in Israel's heritage. A younger son, a child of old age, is often pictured as a favorite son in Old Testament and Rabbinic writings. Roland de Vaux argues that the legislation of Deut. 21:15–17, governing the inheritance laws, gives a double portion to the eldest son, not because he was the favorite, but to protect him against the favoritism often shown the youngest.[67] But even more important for understanding our parable are the stories in which the younger is the favorite. One need only call to mind the stories of Cain and Abel, Ishmael and Isaac, Esau and Jacob, Jacob's favorite son Joseph and, after his supposed death, Benjamin. Genesis 44:18ff. gives a touching account of Jacob's attachment to his younger sons. The cup has been found in Benjamin's bag and Judah begs of Joseph: "We have a father, an old man, and a young brother, the child of his old age; and his brother is dead, and he alone is left of his mother's children; and his father loves him." Other favorite sons are Aaron and Moses and especially David and Solomon, both of whom were the youngest sons. Furthermore this tradition was applied to Israel: "'Is not Esau Jacob's brother?' says the Lord. 'Yet I have loved Jacob but I have hated Esau; I have laid waste his hill country and left his heritage to the jackals of the desert'" (Mal. 1:2–3). Finally, at the Seder meal the youngest son asks the questions of the mighty acts done by God for Israel.

The theme also persists in folklore tradition past New Testament times. An interesting example is preserved in the *Midrash on Psalms*, Ps. 9:1:

> R. Berechiah said in the name of R. Jonathan: . . . the verse means therefore that God has set love of little children in their fathers' hearts. For example, there was a king who had two sons, one grown up, the other a little one. The grown-up one was scrubbed clean, and the little one was covered with dirt, but the king loved the little one more than he loved the grown-up one.[68]

At the beginning of our parable the mention of a father and a younger son reveals the story tradition to which it belongs. The audience knows how it is supposed to be told. According to the tradition of elder and younger son stories, each of the figures will play stereotyped roles. Younger sons are rogues and are forgiven by indulgent fathers. Elder sons, suffering the firstborn's inhibitions, are rejected by the father in favor of the rogue. The test of the storyteller is to provide interesting details around an already known frame of reference.

Lexie 2.   Division (v. 12b)

The younger son requests his father to divide his property among the sons.[69] The father as possessor of the desired object is the subject of the first two lexies. He and he alone can divide the property. He focuses and controls narrative action. By dividing the property he designates the younger son as new subject. The plot will now follow his fate. But a second subject, the elder son, is implied since the father divided the property between *them*. The property's division implies a contract—the younger son will use it to make his fortune, or at least to provide for himself. It is not specified in the parable but is surely implied. If there were no implied contract, the story need not move forward.

Lexie 3.   Departure (v. 13a)

In the previous lexie the father constituted the younger son as subject with an implied contract. The son leaves his father's home to carry out the contract. The parable is well within the traditional two-sons story and likewise within everyday experience. An early division of property was not unusual in Palestine at this period, for opportunities were few and the attractions of the Empire's great cities compelling. Jesus' audience is familiar with such occurrences. Furthermore, in Old Testament stories many younger sons had to leave their father's house to make their way: Isaac had left to find his wife Rebecca; Jacob had fled the wrath of Esau after stealing his brother's birthright; Joseph had made his fortune in Egypt. The audience would have looked favorably upon the son's venture.

Lexie 4.   Loss (v. 13b)

The son immediately aborts his contract to use his share of the property for his well-being. He becomes his own opponent—he squanders his property. No one else is to blame. The institution of the son as his own opponent means that he will have to overcome himself to fulfill his contract. The manner in which he has lost his property, by loose living (*asōtōs*), emphasizes this. From the audience's viewpoint this development is not altogether unexpected, since younger sons are frequently rogues.

Lexie 5.   Famine (v. 14)

A second opponent, famine, depresses the son even more, while drawing sympathy from the audience. At least he is not totally responsible for his sad state.

Lexie 6.   Help? (v. 15)

A helper is offered in the person of a citizen of that land. But even more, the son appears to help himself by going and joining—he moves to get help.

For the audience, however, sympathy and patience with the son is being pushed to the limit. In becoming a swine herder he in effect commits apostasy, for that position was forbidden to Jews.[70] A younger son may be a rogue, but he may not commit apostasy.

Lexie 7.   Hunger (v. 16)

But feeding swine does not benefit him, since he still has nothing to eat. Furthermore he remains his own opponent because he lacks nerve to take the swine's food for his own sustenance.

Lexie 8.   Return (vv. 17–20a)

The son repents of his actions. "To repent" is the meaning of the Aramaic that probably underlies the Greek here translated "He came to himself."[71] By repenting, the son overcomes himself as opponent, alerting the audience that a decisive action is being proposed. The son realizes that his father's servants are better off than he. So if he could only be a servant, his position would improve. He proposes to offer his father a new contract in which he is no longer son but servant. His movement to the father denotes his intention to carry out the plan.

The audience rejoices at this new turn of events. Of course

it does not expect the father to accept the new contract but to restore the old contract, in which the younger son is son. But the son's proposal to be only a servant finds favor in the audience, since it shows that he does not hold his sonship as something he deserves, and this sign of humility reinforces his repentance.

Lexie 9.   Greeting (v. 20b)

The father rushes to become his son's helper. The welcoming scene comes before the son can even speak and confirms the audience's suspicion that the father will not accept a new contract. By kissing and embracing his son, he signals he has forgiven the son.

Lexie 10.   Son's Response (v. 21)

The son attempts to present the father with his new proposal.

Lexie 11.   Father's Response (vv. 22–24a)

The father refuses even to consider the son's new proposal and reinstates the original contract. But what was the original contract? The first apparent contract, which results from a division of the property, stipulates that the son use it for his well-being. But a prior contract is implied at the beginning: "A man had two sons." The contract is "having two sons." The younger son becomes an opponent of this contract when he falls from his father: "Father I have sinned against heaven and before you." Only the father can restore the contract, which he does in this lexie. Thus two stories are present in this first act. The overarching story concerns the father's effort to maintain two sons, and the younger son's story is a sequence threatening to abort the father's story.

For the audience, the father restores the younger son's favorite status. Jeremias has shown that shoes were a sign of luxury and were only worn by free men: "Here they mean that the son must no longer go about barefoot like a slave."[72] He is not to be a servant but a son. Eating meat was a rare event in the East, and a fattened calf was a sign that the feast was of singular importance. Jeremias concludes, "the three orders given by the father manifest tokens of forgiveness and reinstatement."[73] The audience reassures itself. Their positive view of the son is restored. They were not mistaken in their estimate. He is still a favorite. What had started out badly has now been rectified.

Lexie 12.   A Banquet (v. 24b)

The feast confirms the son's restored status and the joy of this restoration. The audience itself comes to the banquet, for they desire to rejoice with the father.

Lexie 13.   Elder Son (v. 25)

Now enters that figure who has haunted the story since his implied existence was mentioned in Lexie 1. Where he has been during the feast is not important and so it is only remarked that he was in the field, out of range. For the audience this is appropriate because the elder son will play a negative role and his presence for the celebration would have spoiled it. Because of a stereotyped role assigned him, he does not enter the party, but only hears the music and dancing.

Lexie 14.   Report (vv. 26–27)

A servant's report serves to bring the brother up to date on his younger brother's situation and to postpone the inevitable scene where the elder son will act out his role as villain. The postponement heightens the audience's expectation. The lexie also provides the elder son an opportunity to celebrate with his father the return of his younger brother.

Lexie 15.   Response (v. 28a)

The anger and rejection is expected. The elder brother is clearly a villain. His response means that he is unwilling to ratify the father's restoration of the younger son. By refusing to accept his brother back, he is threatening his father's having two sons. The elder brother's anger is a sign that he has cut himself off from his brother, leaving his father to choose between them.

Lexie 16.   A Plea (v. 28b)

From the audience's viewpoint the father becomes a foil by which the elder son is confirmed in his role as villain and then rejected. But there is also another possibility. The elder son's anger threatens the father's two sons and so his entreaty is an attempt to ratify his own contract. The father would once again have two sons.

Lexie 17.   Retort (vv. 29–30)

The elder son lives up to his advance billing. His response is in marked contrast to that of his younger brother upon his return home. The younger had come as a penitent; the elder comes complaining that he has not received his just due. He also compares himself to his brother. He has been faithful, followed the father's command; his brother wasted his father's living with harlots. He questions his father's response to his sons. To the faithless son the father has been more than generous; to the faithful one he has given nothing. His rejection of his brother is quite clear when he refers to "this son of yours." The younger son is not his brother, but his father's son.

The elder brother's complaint is correct. There is no indication that his summary is unfair. But this is beside the point because the elder brother is following his script. The audience views him as a scoundrel, for that is their tradition. This elder son is a successor to Cain, Ishmael, and Esau.

Lexie 18.   Response (v. 31)

This is a crushing blow for the audience. Instead of being punished, the elder son inherits all ("All that is mine is yours"). The story is not supposed to end this way according to the audience's tradition. At a narrative level the father accomplishes two things with the response. By announcing that his son is always with him he refuses to accept any excuse for separating his sons from himself. Just as the father would not listen to the younger when he only wanted to be a servant, so now when the elder attempts to withdraw, the father blocks it. The second part of the response affirms the elder son as heir of the father's property, leaving the audience in a quandary. How can all be given to the elder son if the father has forgiven and reinstated the younger son? The audience has been deceived: the elder son's expected rejection has not occurred. Even more, he has been acknowledged as heir.

Lexie 19. Celebration (v. 32)

This verse is problematical. Previously it concluded the younger son's scene and here turns attention back to that first part, which is where Luke saw the emphasis. For this reason it is possible that Luke repeated the verse as a conclusion to the parable. But even if the verse is secondary, it does not do violence to the parable if one sees it as raising a question. If, however, one sees it as overcoming the previous verse, then violence has been done.

The story can be heard from two different points of view. From the tradition of stories about younger and elder sons, the subjects are the sons. But in retelling this tradition, the parable has instituted a new subject, the father. That this is the case can be seen from the parable's structure. The story begins with "A certain man had two sons." There follows the first sequence in which the younger son attempts to use his share of the property for his betterment. In this sequence the younger son is subject, but it aborts when he fails. He must return to his father to accomplish his well-being. So in the final part of the first act the father becomes subject restoring his son. In the second sequence the elder son becomes the subject who seeks to destroy the father's acceptance of the younger son. He presents the father with a choice: me or him. The father refuses the choice by himself becoming subject and confirming sonship and property on the elder son. Unsuccessful contracts are attempted by the sons; successful contracts by the father. He is the overarching subject of the parable.

The careful use of terms defining relationships points to the father as the overarching subject. Attention was called to this feature in analyzing Lexie 1. The father has two sons (*duō hyious*). This may best be translated in English as "two heirs" since it is not their maleness that is important, but that they are heirs. Immediately one of the sons is identified as "younger" (*neōteros*, v. 12). *Neōteros* implies the existence of *presbyteros*.[74] As was argued above, these explicit references are part of the parable's economy, recalling to mind an explicit tradition. At the conclusion of the first sequence, the father refers to the

younger as "this my son" (*houtos ho hyios mou*, v. 24). This will
contrast with the elder son's reply. In v. 25 the elder son is
introduced with his appropriate technical designation: *presbyteros*. In arguing with his father, the elder son refers to his
brother as "this son of yours" (*ho hyios sou houtos*), a con-
temptuous use of *houtos*.[75] The elder son thus implicitly denies
his relationship with his brother. The father responds to this
attack with the vocative, "dear child" (*teknon*). The vocative is
regularly used as sign of affection.[76] This affective use of the vocative destroys the legal relation between heir and father as well
as the rivalry between siblings. It insists that the relation of child
to father is primary.

The parable calls upon the audience to hear an old story
from a new viewpoint, the father's. Furthermore, in retelling
the tradition is modified. The father loves both equally and refuses to choose between them, confirming each in turn as sons.

One of the theses we have isolated as representing a segment
of the phenomenal World of parables concerns the congruity of
the secular and the religious (Thesis III). Here we have a variation on this theme. The traditional story of two sons functions
on at least two levels. The conflict between brothers is a traditional folklore tale which is probably dependent upon psychological mechanisms. The parable retells this story, but by insti-
tuting the father as subject it draws attention away from the
breach between brothers and turns it instead toward a father
who refuses to lose his sons. Basically, the parable heals wounds
deep within the human soul. To enter the parable's World is to
accept its healing power. It demands the rejection of a viewpoint of brother against brother and the acceptance of the father's
viewpoint where healing is a necessity. If healing does not take
place, then the father's fathership is destroyed. That is how it is
in Kingdom. Kingdom is an act of healing and to deny its healing powers is to reject and destroy it.

On a second level the parable is also a retelling of Israel's
history insofar as elements of that history have been symbolized
within the framework of a two-sons tradition. This does not
mean that the parable is an allegory of Israel's history. But significant parts of Israel's own history involve the tradition being

retold, and even Israel herself is identified with the tradition (Mal. 1:2–3). To enter the parable is to reconsider the function of this tradition upon Israel's self-understanding. If the two-sons tradition has been used to separate Israel, to mark her out as chosen among the nations, there is, along with the healing power of this parable, a universalism implicitly present. The parable admits the equal status of both elder and younger as the father's children. Within Israel's context this is a challenge to universalism. The parable uses a traditional secular image to reweave into a new fabric the elements of Israel's self-understanding.

Grace is a major theme in the parable and should afford an opportunity to sharpen observations made about grace in previous parables (Thesis II). In the Samaritan's parable the thesis concerning grace was formulated to focus upon the individual who receives grace. To receive grace one must have no alternative. The present parable presents in the two sons examples of being graced. The younger receives grace of sonship when he has fallen so far that the only way he can go is up. His case is analogous to that of the man in the ditch, a classic case of grace.

The elder son is more complicated. The traditional characterization of him as self-righteous is not without foundation in the parable, as we have seen. Therefore, how can he qualify for grace under the analogy of the man in the ditch? The elder son, as the traditional villain, is cut off from grace by the story's very form. When the father changes the ending of the traditional story by refusing to allow him to reject his own sonship, the son is offered grace. As villain the elder son does not want grace nor does the audience wish him to receive it. But in one aspect the elder son is like the man in the ditch; he is forced into his role as villain. Grace allows him to step out of that role. The man in the ditch likewise had no choice about entering the ditch—he was beaten up and robbed, a passive agent. So too with the elder brother. Grace is also offered the audience in the figure of the elder brother, if only they acknowledge that what the father has done is the way it is in Kingdom. To accept grace they must be willing to surrender their own ending for the story and accept it as parable. Grace, as the parable's offering, is the last alternative: for the younger son that he may return to his father's house as a son; for the elder brother that he may at last step out of the demands of playing the role of elder brother; for the audience that they may acknowledge that to accept the elder brother is the Kingdom of God.

A comic vision under the guise of tragedy thoroughly permeates this parable (Thesis I). Both sons are presented as tragic figures; they both fall; and the father raises them both. But to an even greater extent the father risks tragedy, a tragedy of death, for to lose his sons would be to kill him as father. He no longer would be a father, but simply a man. He refuses to draw tragic conclusions from his children's acts; he accepts them regardless of what they have done. In this parable when the comic appears under the guise of tragedy, tragedy is not avoided, but is real. The younger son is lost, and the attack of the elder brother is painful. But pain is accepted in order to manifest grace for the sons.

By using the five theses elaborated above to organize our discussion, we have been able to show that these four narrative parables share a number of common themes. In turn, the analysis of each parable has given greater precision to the theses so that now each thesis represents a variety of moments within our corpus of parables. Much like a piece of music we have developed variations on a theme. In the next chapter we will pursue the variations with parables of a different type.

NOTES

1. The English word "parable" presents problems in the discussion of parables because the word has its own history in English usage. According to the *Oxford English Dictionary* "parable" is equivalent to "allegory." This unconscious assumption means that when the critic defines a "parable" over against "allegory," a technical term is created that is at variance with normal usage.

2. For a summary of the usage of *parabolē* and *mashal* see Friedrich Hauck, "*parabolē*," *Theological Dictionary of the New Testament*, hereinafter *TDNT*, ed. Gerhard Kittel, trans. Geoffrey W. Bromiley

(Grand Rapids: Eerdmans, 1968), 5: esp. 744–51. For recent review, see Madeleine Boucher, *The Mysterious Parable*, Catholic Biblical Quarterly—Monograph Series (Washington, D.C.: Catholic Biblical Association of America, 1977), pp. 86–89.

3. *Die Gleichnisreden Jesu* (Darmstadt: Wissenschaftliche Buchgesellschaft, 1969; first published 1899–1910), pp. 49ff. Jülicher's significance lies in his centering attention upon the Jewish *mashal*, thereby destroying the Hellenistic allegory. Joachim Jeremias, *The Parables of Jesus*, trans. H. S. Hooke (New York: Charles Scribner's Sons, 1963), pp. 18–19, evaluates Jülicher's contribution. For Jeremias, Jülicher's positive gain was his destruction of allegorical interpretation; his error was his seeking to draw "from each [of the parables] a single idea of the widest possible generality."

4. Bultmann, *History of the Synoptic Tradition*, hereinafter, *HST*, trans. John Marsh (New York: Harper and Row, 1963), p. 174, borrows Jülicher's distinction.

5. E.g., ibid, p. 175; C. H. Dodd, *The Parables of the Kingdom* (New York: Charles Scribner's Sons, 1961), p. 7.

6. Robert Funk, "The Good Samaritan as Metaphor," *Semeia* 2 (1974): 76.

7. E.g., Robert Funk, *Language, Hermeneutic and the Word of God*, hereinafter, *LHWG* (New York: Harper and Row, 1966), chap. 5; John Dominic Crossan, *In Parables* (New York: Harper and Row, 1973), pp. 10–16.

8. This distinction reduces in practice Jülicher's three groups to two, similitude and parable, except that I understand both as properly parables.

9. Jeremias, *Parables of Jesus*, chap. 2, still remains a masterful survey of the problem involved in the preservation of the parables.

10. Crossan, *In Parables*, pp. 115–20, attempts to overcome this problem by a structural analysis of two groups of Servant parables. As interesting as Crossan's analysis is, it is hampered because his two groups contradict each other. Since no chronological relation between the "Servant parables" can be established, the development of teller's thought remains a mystery.

11. Mary Ann Tolbert, *Perspectives on the Parables* (Philadelphia: Fortress Press, 1979), p. 20, opposes the reconstructive task. I find her opposition ill-founded and one of a number of major methodological problems in her work.

12. Dan O. Via, *The Parables* (Philadelphia: Fortress Press, 1967), pp. 18–25, glories in this, especially in his usage of the New Criti-

cism's dictum that "criticism is not biography." The parables are aesthetic objects, but a reliable knowledge of Jesus' context would surely help clarify important points of debate.

13. Ibid.; Funk, *LHWG*, p. 177.

14. I have titled the parables simply from the first line for two reasons: (1) the traditional titles frequently encapsulate an allegorical interpretation or (2) attempts to give titles are reductions to a "point." Originally parables did not have titles.

15. *HST*, p. 178. Perrin, *Jesus and the Language of the Kingdom* (Philadelphia: Fortress Press, 1976), chap. 3, uses the "Good Samaritan" as a case study, presenting a summary and critique of recent scholarship of this parable.

16. *Parables of Jesus*, p. 202.

17. Crossan, *In Parables*, p. 59, convincingly argues for this twofold understanding of neighbor.

18. Funk, "The Good Samaritan as Metaphor," p. 79.

19. The audience is implied in the text, in fact, is part of its repertoire. Without the convention of first-century Judaism the text would become opaque. See Wolfgang Iser, *The Act of Reading* (Baltimore: Johns Hopkins University Press, 1978), esp. pp. 20–85.

20. The analysis is of the narrative structure. For further details see Daniel Patte, *What Is Structural Exegesis?* Guides to Biblical Scholarship (Philadelphia: Fortress Press, 1976); idem, "An Analysis of Narrative Structure and the Good Samaritan," *Semeia* 2 (1974): 1–26. I have modified the methodology toward simplicity and intelligibility.

21. Jeremias, *Parables of Jesus*, p. 203.

22. Both Patte, "An Analysis of Narrative Structure," p. 14, and Funk, "Samaritan as Metaphor," p. 77, from different methodological viewpoints maintain the man as victim is subject.

23. Funk, ibid., p. 78 and *LHWG*, p. 212, argue that the audience identifies with the man in the ditch. But this is not so: they are in sympathy; identification is normally reserved for the hero/helper.

24. Jeremias, *Parables of Jesus*, p. 204. Jeremias rightly rejects speculation as to why the priest and Levite "pass by." For the parable the reason is unimportant.

25. Jeremias, *Parables of Jesus*, p. 205.

26. K. H. Rengstorf, *"lēstēs," TDNT* 4: 261, suggests that the bandits are zealots, since the Greek word is frequently used for them. Given the specific identification of the other characters, his suggestion is tempting. The parallelism between zealot/bandit and Samaritan/hero would be quite interesting. From the zealot viewpoint, the pairing should be the opposite.

27. One should recall Paul Ricoeur's warning ("Biblical Hermeneutics," *Semeia* 4 [1975]: 33), that the parables are not simply artful stories, but their meaning effect is to be found as qualified by the symbol Kingdom of God.

28. Cf. Via, *The Parables*, pp. 96ff. Via has continued to mine this distinction in his book *Kerygma and Comedy in the New Testament* (Philadelphia: Fortress Press, 1975).

29. "The structure, shape, and interconnections of an allegory are determined by something outside itself" (ibid., pp. 4–8). Via refers to allegory as the twice-told tale.

30. Eta Linnemann, *Jesus of the Parables*, trans. John Sturdy (New York: Harper and Row, 1966), pp. 88–97, assumes the reconstruction to be so simple that she deals with variations at the end of her exegesis.

31. Bultmann, *HST*, p. 175.

32. *Parables of Jesus*, p. 63; Wolfgang Trilling, *Das Wahre Israel*, Studien zum Alten and Neuen Testament 10 (Munich: Kösel Verlag, 1964), pp. 84ff. Charles Carlston, *The Parables of the Triple Tradition* (Philadelphia: Fortress Press, 1975), pp. 40–41, deals with Matthew's redactional intention in Matt. 21:23—22:22; Funk, *LHWG*, pp. 168–72; A. Ogawa, "Paraboles de l'Israel véritable? Reconsidération critique de Mt. xxi 28–xxii 14," *Novum Testamentum* 21 (1979): 124–49.

33. Günther Bornkamm, "End-Expectation and Church in Matthew," in Bornkamm, Barth, and Held, *Tradition and Interpretation in Matthew*, trans. Percy Scott (London: SCM Press, 1963), p. 20.

34. Jeremias, *Parables of Jesus*, p. 64.

35. Funk, *LHWG*, p. 184.

36. Jesus said: A man had guest-friends, and when he had prepared the dinner, he sent his servant to invite the guest-friends. He went to the first, he said to him: "My master invites thee." He said: "I have some claims against some merchants; they will come to me in the evening; I will go and give them my orders. I pray to be excused from the dinner." He went to another, he said to him: "My master has invited thee." He said to him: "I have bought a house and they request me for a day. I will have no time." He came to another, he said to him: "My master invites thee." He said to him: "My friend is to be married and I am to arrange a dinner; I shall not be able to come. I pray to be excused from the dinner." He went to another, he said to him: "My master invites thee." He said to him: "I have bought a farm, I go to collect the rent. I shall not be able to come. I pray to be excused." The servant came, he said to his master: "Those whom thou hast invited to the dinner have excused themselves." The mas-

ter said to his servant: "Go out to the roads, bring those whom thou shalt find, so that they may dine. Tradesmen and merchants shall not [enter] the places of my Father."

(From *The Gospel According to Thomas*, Coptic text established and translated by A. Guillaumont, H. Ch. Puech, G. Quispel, W. Till and Yassah 'Abd Al Masih [New York: Harper and Row, 1959], Logion 64.)

37. Bultmann, *HST*, p. 191.

38. Jeremias, *Parables of Jesus*, p. 176.

39. Ibid., p. 177.

40. Ibid., p. 176.

41. Exclusion of vv. 21b–22 is explained above, p. 34.

42. Jeremias, *Parables of Jesus*, p. 176.

43. Funk, *LHWG*, p. 190, sees the burlesque leading the story over the border of the everyday into a world of fantasy.

44. Jeremias argues that the purpose of the banquet was originally to improve the master's social status. This may be true, but his interpretation is based upon seeing this parable as a variant of a rabbinic one whose conclusion deals with the one good deed of a tax collector. Once a tax collector had given a party for the city counselors which they refused to attend. Instead he invited the poor. For Jeremias, the man of the Jesus parable is a tax collector. Nothing in the present story demands such a supposition.

45. Via, *The Parables*, pp. 113f.

46. E.g, Bultmann, *HST*, p. 195; Jeremias, *Parables of Jesus*, p. 59.

47. Jeremias, *Parables of Jesus*, p. 59.

48. This section is part of the eschatological discourse whose theme is set out at Matt. 24:37: "As were the days of Noah, so will be the coming of the Son of man." Then, a series of parables deals with the Lord of the Parousia. Immediately following the parable of the talents is Matthew's description of the final judgment.

49. This is a favorite phrase of Matthew's (8:21; 13:24, 50; 22:13; 24:51).

50. Bultmann, *HST*, p. 176. The parallel with Luke shows that this dominical logion had already been added to the parable in Q.

51. Via, *The Parables*, pp. 101–2, argues that the symmetrical form of the plot is derived from its tragic character—the downward fall of the one-talent man.

52. Ibid., p. 115.

53. Jeremias, *Parables of Jesus*, p. 60.

54. Via, *The Parables*, p. 119, also sees this response as rejecting the servant's characterization of the master, thereby exposing the servant's responsibility for his own tragic situation.

55. Ibid., p. 100. Via sees the subject as the third servant, since his tragic fall defines the plot.

56. In the Lucan version this expectation is made explicit: "Trade with these till I come" (v. 13b).

57. The audience in Luke (v. 25) does protest. This verse clearly shows the powerful hold of the stereotype upon the imagination. The textual problem with the verse only serves to accentuate this; cf. A *Textual Commentary on the New Testament*, ed. Bruce M. Metzger (New York: United Bible Societies, 1971), p. 169.

58. This attack on the stereotype may be related to Jesus' rejection of apocalyptic ideology. Likewise, the master's positive image should be borne in mind when discussing Jesus' association with the outcast and poor.

59. Via, *The Parables*, p. 116.

60. I have dealt with the controlling influence of the Lucan context on the interpretation of the parable in "The Prodigal Son: A Structuralist Interpretation," *Semeia* 9 (1977): 45–48. See further I. Broer, "Das Gleichnis vom verlorenen Sohn und die Theologie des Lukas," *New Testament Studies* 20 (1974): 453–62 and the reaction of L. Ramaroson, "Le Coeur du Troisième Évangile: Lc 15," *Biblica* 60 (1979): 348–60.

61. Jeremias, *Parables of Jesus*, p. 131.

62. The interpretative accent upon the first part has led to a challenge of the integrity of the second part. C. Carlston, "Reminiscence and Redaction in Luke 15:11–32," *Journal of Biblical Literature* 94 (1975): 368–90, has shown the integrity of the parable beyond reasonable doubt. For a summary of the debate prior to the publication of Carlston's article, see my paper prepared for the Society of Biblical Literature's Parables Seminar in *Seminar Papers: 1975* (Missoula: Scholars Press, 1975), pp. 186–91.

63. Jeremias, *Parables of Jesus*, p. 131.

64. Ibid., p. 132.

65. Ibid., p. 129. Jeremias argues that because the property already has been divided (v. 12b), v. 31 correctly indicates that the elder brother is the sole heir.

66. "The first sentence of the parable does not yet reveal to Jesus' hearers in what direction he is going." Linnemann, *Jesus of the Parables*, p. 74.

67. Roland de Vaux, *Ancient Israel* (New York: McGraw-Hill, 1961), p. 42.

68. *Midrash on Psalms*, trans. W. G. Braude, Yale Judaica Series 13 (New Haven: Yale University Press, 1959), p. 131. L. Schottroff, "Das Gleichnis vom verlorenen Sohn," *Zeitschrift für Theologie und Kirche* 68 (1971): 44, also notes this rabbinic parallel but dismisses it. Paul, in Gal. 4:22ff., uses this tradition in the allegory of Abraham's two sons. In that allegory the elder son Ishmael stands for the children of slavery, the present Jerusalem, and the younger son, Isaac, for the children of freedom, the heavenly Jerusalem. "Now we, brethren, like Isaac, are children of Promise" (4:28).

69. D. Daube, "Inheritance in Two Lukan Pericopes," *Zeitschrift der Savigny-Stiftung für Rechtsgeschichte* 72 (1955): 334, has shown that the situation depicted is realistic in terms of Palestinian customs.

70. Jeremias, *Parables of Jesus*, p. 129, who quotes b.B.Q. 82b, "Cursed be the man who breeds swine."

71. Ibid.

72. Ibid., p. 130.

73. Ibid.

74. G. Bornkamm, "*presbus*," *TDNT* 6: 652, gives the evidence for showing the implied relationship. *Neōteros* alone means "young"; *presbyteros* alone means "old." The comparative sense normally comes into play only with the expression of the other term.

75. Jeremias, *Parables*, p. 131; Walter Bauer, *A Greek-English Lexicon of the New Testament*, hereinafter *BAG*, trans. William Arndt and Wilber Gingrich, 2d rev. ed. by Gingrich and Frederick W. Danker (Chicago: University of Chicago Press, 1979), p. 597.

76. *BAG*, p. 808; Albrecht Oepke, "*pais*," *TDNT* 5:638.

3

ONE-LINERS

While Kingdom of God is the unexpressed referent of narrative parables, in three of the parables to be considered in this chapter—Mustard Seed, Leaven, and Seed Cast upon the Ground—it is the expressed referent. We should expect, therefore, to develop greater precision regarding Kingdom in Jesus' language. If by means of the five theses developed in the previous chapter we can show the phenomenal World of these parables to be identical with the narrative parables, we will have confirmed the position of modern scholarship that Kingdom is the implied referent of narrative parables.

Before we can move to this question, we first must clarify the formal status of these parables as *meshalim*. There are obvious formal differences between parables in the synoptic tradition. How to classify those differences on the basis of objective criteria has been a perplexing problem ever since Jülicher's pioneering attempts.[1] As we saw in the previous chapter, the distinction between parable proper and example story was based not upon something inherent in form but on a presumed subjective interpretation. Likewise, there are problems associated with the distinction between similitude and parable.

For Jülicher similitudes were similes: "The Kingdom of God is like . . . ." Parables proper were narratives in which the figurative element had undergone elaboration. The common-sense observation of difference between a simple sentence and an extended narrative needs to be remembered. As numerous commentators have noticed, however, the actual line between similitude and parable proper is often difficult to draw.[2] The difficulty arises when this distinction is made on the basis of

simile rather than on the basis of the relation of similitude to
mashal.

Jeremias has argued that the introductory formula used in
similitudes should be translated not "it is like," but "it is the case
with . . . as with . . . ."[3] The Greek introductory dative is dependent upon an Aramaic *l*[c] formula. Jeremias's clue is important,
but he himself did not follow it up. He still interprets similitudes
as similes because he seeks a single point of comparison. "The
kingdom of God is, of course, not 'like a merchant' but like a
pearl."[4]

The quest for a single point destroys a parable's metaphorical
character. Amos Wilder argued that the so-called Kingdom parables are not true similes,[5] and following this suggestion Robert
Funk maintained there was no single point. Rather, "if the parable is a genuine metaphor, it is more likely that the parable *as a
whole* is to be brought into relation to the subject."[6] Funk's observation is of decisive methodological importance. As metaphors, narrative parables and similitudes operate in exactly the
same fashion. It is not "Kingdom of God is like . . . ." but
"Kingdom of God *is* . . . ." Kingdom as symbol is brought into
conjunction with an image created by the metaphor, and that
conjunction is the moment of meaning.

The real difference between similitudes and narrative parables
lies at a different level than Jülicher's grammatical distinction.
To indicate this, I will call them "one-liners" because they are
also related to another type of *mashal*, the proverb. They share
a metaphorical structure with narrative parables, while having
the style of a proverb. Both Bultmann and Dodd hinted at this
in their discussions, but failed to develop it. Bultmann placed
the difference between narratives and similitudes in the "typical
condition, or typical, recurrent event."[7] Dodd also noticed that
in Jesus' figurative language "the germ of the parable is already
present."[8]

William A. Beardslee's pioneering work on proverbs allows us
to follow up Dodd's suggestion.[9] Beardslee points out that both
parables and proverbs are wisdom forms[10] and he detects a relationship between parable and proverb. There is a "close connection between proverb and story."[11] A proverb presupposes a story
of human experience of which it is the distillation. It "is a state-

ment about a particular kind of occurrence or situation, an orderly tract of experience which can be repeated."[12] The presupposed story is that tract of experience from which "a cluster of insights" is drawn.[13] The function of proverbial insight is to create a "continuous whole out of one's existence."[14]

According to Beardslee, synoptic proverbs characteristically intensify and concentrate wisdom. A strategy for this is paradox and hyperbole.[15] So intense is the reversal that "the imagination is jolted out of its vision of a continuous connection between one situation and the other."[16] These proverbs destroy proverbial logic because they challenge the presuppositions of the story supporting proverb as a cluster of insights, the presupposition that one can make a complete story out of existence. Precisely this challenge to a common-sense way of life becomes a way of life. Proverb uses this challenge "to jolt the reader into a new insight."[17]

The parables to be considered in this chapter are parabolic proverbs. I have chosen to call these "one-liners" on the analogy of one-line jokes. They share with the proverbs intensification and concentration of language, but they are parables because their intensified language, with its implied proverbial story, is a metaphor for the symbol Kingdom of God. The metaphorical association effects meaning. Instead of summarizing an insight, one-liners use intensified insight as a metaphor for Kingdom to create a World of new meaning for the hearer.

For narrative parables, narrative motion provided the vehicle for metaphor. In one-liners, intensified insight is metaphor's vehicle.

In this chapter we will follow the same procedure as previously. Following the isolation of redactional usage, we will "read" the parable. Finally, we will relate the parable to the five theses developed above. Because these parables do not function as narrative metaphors, but as proverbial metaphors, we should expect a gain in understanding.

MUSTARD PLANT

Dominic Crossan has provided a fine form critical analysis of this parable, to which the following is greatly indebted.[18] Although this parable has come down in the synoptic tradition at Mark 4:30–32, Matt. 13:31–32, and Luke 13:18–19, they are not three independent versions. Mark as a source of Matthew and Luke is one source and, as will be shown, Matthew and Luke have available also a Q version. There is likewise a non-canonical version in the Gospel of Thomas (logion 20). So there are three versions within the tradition. Recovering the parable's most probable original form will involve an examination of Mark to determine redactional elements, a reconstruction of a Q version, and finally a comparison with Thomas.

The Marcan parable is redundant. "A grain of mustard seed, which *when sown* upon ground, is the smallest of all seeds on earth; yet *when it is sown* . . . ." Besides the obvious two sowings, likewise "upon the ground" and "on the earth" is redundant. It would appear that Mark has added the last part of each redundancy. Crossan argues that redundancy is characteristic of the Marcan insertion technique, i.e., when Mark inserts something into his text he frequently rephrases the text after the insertion.[19] On the basis of this stylistic pattern, Crossan concludes that the Marcan insertion is the note concerning the mustard seed being the smallest of all seeds. If this is so, then the reference to the greatest of all shrubs is also from Mark. According to Crossan, Mark inserted into the parable the contrast between smallest and greatest.[20]

The Lucan version (which is probably following Q very closely, in contrast to the Matthean text, which is a conflation of both Q and Mark)[21] confirms major aspects of Crossan's reconstruction. Luke has no mention of the comparison between smallest and greatest. A basic difference between Luke and Mark concerns the parable's ending. Mark's reconstructed conclusion would read: "It grows up and becomes a shrub and puts forth large branches so that the birds of the air can make nests in its shade." In Luke, the mustard seed grows up to become "a tree, and the birds of the air made nests in its branches." Crossan maintains that the Lucan form is secondary, since a mustard plant, when mature, is not a tree but a shrub.[22] With the tree have come birds, making their nests in its branches rather than its shade.

The version in the Gospel of Thomas raises further problems for a reconstruction of the original.

The disciples said to Jesus: Tell us what the Kingdom of Heaven is like. He said to them: It is like a mustard seed, smaller than all seeds. But when it falls on the tilled earth, it produces a large branch and becomes shelter for the birds of heaven.

The superlative contrast between the smallest and greatest is missing, although there is a reference to its smallness and its putting forth a great branch. Likewise, what it grows into is not specified. The Greek word *skepē*, which survives only in Thomas, means primarily "shelter," but also has a derived meaning, "shade."[23]

The following chart indicates the differences we have observed.

MARK	Q	THOMAS
seed smallest	————————	smaller than
greatest	————————	large branch
shrub	tree	————————
nests in shade	nests in branches	shelter/shade

These observations provide a perspective for a tentative reconstruction of the original. While the superlative contrast (smallest/greatest) is clearly from Mark, should one agree with Crossan that the original parable probably contained a reference to smaller and great along the lines suggested by Thomas?[24] Two observations tell against this suggestion. Not only does Q fail to contain any such reference, but also the mustard seed's proverbial smallness surely would have suggested the reference in the course of the oral tradition.[25] Further, "great branch" in Thomas finds its parallel in Mark not in "the greatest of all shrubs," but in "puts forth large branches." Finally, that Mark's reference to nesting in the shade is original is confirmed by the ambiguous usage (shelter/shade) of Thomas.

If these suggestions are accepted, the original form would be something like the following:

It is like a grain of mustard seed, which, when sown upon the ground, grows up and becomes a shrub and puts forth large branches, so that the birds of the air can make nests in its shade.

Why has such an apparently simple parable had such a con-voluted history? Why the reference to "the greatest of all shrubs"? Why did Q call it a "tree"?

Crossan suggests that this results from aligning the text with the Old Testament tradition of the Apocalyptic Tree.[26] There are three possible texts to refer to: Ps. 104:12, Dan. 4:10–12, and Ezek. 17:23. The first two can be dismissed, for in the Psalm birds sing and in Daniel the tree is a reference to Pharaoh of Egypt. But the Ezekiel text is striking. "On the mountain height of Israel will I plant it, that it may bring forth boughs and bear fruit, and become a noble cedar; and under it will dwell all kinds of beasts; in the shade of its branches birds of every sort will nest." For Crossan the Ezekiel text did not influence the original para-ble, but he does argue that the image of the Great Tree has im-plicitly determined the development of shrub into tree. "When one starts a parable with a mustard seed, one cannot end it with a tree, much less the great apocalyptic tree, unless, of course, one plans to lampoon rather rudely the whole apocalyptic tradi-tion."[27] But what Crossan fails to account for is why three inde-pendent versions should include some reference to the Great Tree of Ezekiel if the original parable contained no hints of it. If, normally, mustard seed is not associated with the Great Tree, why did the tradition make such an association? If the original conclusion of the parable is similar to the one preserved in Mark, then Q's change from shrub to tree is comprehensible only on the basis that the original contained an implicit reference to Ezekiel.

There is another consideration that indicates the original par-able did have an intended reference to Ezekiel. The proverbial story (in Beardslee's sense) that lies behind this parabolic proverb is the common-sense observation of growth. As Crossan has pointed out, the ancient mind imagined growth as an example of God's miracle.[28] Paul's use of the seed analogy to explain the resurrection of the body in 1 Cor. 15:35–44 is an example.[29] Crossan is right in seeing the accent falling upon the notion of miracle, of God's gift within Kingdom. The ancient mind did not stress biological development, but divine intervention.

Although Crossan has the metaphor's basic elements correct,

he inadvertently overlooked a deeper symbolism. Why does the parable use a mustard seed as vehicle? If the significance is in miracle, why specify what kind of seed? In the parable of the sower the type of seed is apparently of no importance, and so not specified. Mark possibly saw this and inserted the comparison of the smallest and the greatest. But mustard seed, while a traditional example of smallness, does not grow into the largest of anything. Mark's insertion alerts us to the fact that the detail of mustard seed is not a mere accident, but calls for explanation.

Why the seed is a mustard seed appears in the conclusion, which recalls the Great Tree of Ezekiel. Instead of Kingdom being compared to a Great Tree it is compared to a mustard plant. From the hearer's viewpoint the parable demands a change of story at the end. A mustard seed at the beginning probably implies a story of growth dealing with the theme of smallness. The tradition tried to supply this story. But the original conclusion, with its reference to the Great Tree, introduces another story, one at variance with that expected of the mustard seed.[30] When the two stories are juxtaposed with the symbol Kingdom of God, a possibility for parabolic insight is created.

The element of miracle within the parable should have been taken for granted, even though it has not been. Just as the seed is God's miracle, so also is Kingdom. In Ezekiel, God plants the tree. So miracle is intrinsic within the Kingdom's sphere. But parable as a focus of vision guides one to the miracle. The implicit contrast between the mustard seed and the Great Tree raises the question of an appropriate image for Kingdom. What does it say about Kingdom to use a mustard seed as its image rather than a Great Tree? It not only makes fun of the apocalyptic tradition with its exaggerated expectations, but carries with it the threat that Kingdom may be so ordinary that it will be missed.[31] It is a miracle, but how big a miracle?

We are now in a position to relate this parable to our theses about the underlying World of narrative parables. One-liners, while having the same metaphorical structure as narrative parables, are also related to proverb. Does this change indicate a shift in phenomenal World? Can our previous theses be used to represent the World of these parables? Furthermore, in these parables, Kingdom of God is the metaphor's explicit referent. This means that Kingdom as metaphorically present in parables should become more evident.

Crossan's isolation of the theme of miracle suggests that grace is likewise a primary topic of the parable. In narrative parables, grace comes to those who have no other alternative (Thesis II). But since the parable has no characters, such a personalistic thesis is inappropriate. But is the implied understanding of grace the same for the two types of parables? Where is grace manifest?

The parable centers attention upon mustard seed, which, as a comical burlesque of the Great Tree, demands that the hearer accept grace in an unexpected fashion. The Kingdom's miracle, its grace, demands the acknowledgment that indeed the mustard seed is the appropriate metaphor. The Great Tree of Ezekiel conjures up power, greatness, and magnificence. The mustard seed conjures up a contrary image. To accept the mustard seed is to get into the ditch.

Can the thesis on grace be more clearly formulated? In comparison with the Samaritan, this parable calls for one to accept grace under the guise of the insignificant. For the recipient, Kingdom may be the only alternative left (one must be in the ditch; the Samaritan will minister); in its appearance Kingdom may not be overly obvious. The parable turns attention to an apparently insignificant shrub and says this is the Kingdom of God.

In the parable religious and secular are congruous (Thesis III). The use of a natural metaphor indicates the secular is a model for the religious. Also by rejecting the Great Tree allegory and pointing to a mustard seed in its *natural* environment, the parable refuses to accept the natural world as simply a steno-symbolic substitute for the religious. God is not an actor in the parable as he was in the Ezekiel passage. What is described is a mustard seed's normal growth pattern. The parable has no supernatural overlay.

Finally, is the comic manifested under the guise of tragedy (Thesis I)? Surely the mustard seed does not risk tragedy to gain a comic ending. It is those who are parabled, the hearer and the teller. The teller must risk tragedy in proclaiming this image of his vision. Is he right in rejecting the traditional image? He risks tragedy because the audience may reject his perception. The hearer takes the same risk in accepting the mustard seed, for he must abandon the tradition, the way he has known, and place faith in a much less impressive phenomenon. Such metaphor for Kingdom is truly revolutionary and unprecedented, for it seeks to reverse the hearer's normal expectation. It removes those normal moorings that help to identify reality, and asks instead that the hearer enter a journey with the parable teller. How dare one compare the mighty ruling activity of God to the growth (albeit miraculous) of mustard seed!

LEAVEN
(Matthew 13:33, Luke 13:20–21)

One wonders at first glance how such a simple sentence can be called a parable. Is it not simply a description of an everyday event? How can comparing Kingdom to mixing leaven in flour be either parabolic or illuminating? Jeremias's response to such commonness is to take the leaven's working as an example of how Kingdom develops. "Out of the most insignificant beginnings, invisible to the human eye, God creates his mighty kingdom, which embraces all the people of the world."[32] This interpretation depends upon seeing the Mustard Seed and Leaven as correlative, so that they say one and the same thing.[33] However, Jeremias saw the Mustard Seed's significance in a contrast between the seed's smallness and the greatness of its branches. Since this element is secondary, Jeremias's interpretation has been led astray by Mark's redaction. For Jeremias the parable is not truly parabolic, since he finds no difficulty in reducing its meaning to a propositional statement, thereby expressing the incomprehensible as comprehensible. In his hands parable is transformed into example story.

But, if one listens to the parable its everydayness begins to dissolve. The resonances are there for those who have ears to hear!

Funk contends that to say that the woman took and *hid* leaven in the meal sounds strange, even to those who read the parable

in English.[34] Dodd suggests leaven is hidden in that at first
nothing appears to happen.[35] But the emphasis does not fall upon
leaven (read allegorically "Kingdom") being hidden, but that a
woman hides the leaven. Her activity is described. The leaven is
deliberately made to disappear. Funk ties this into the Jesus
tradition where the Kingdom is spoken of as hidden, and suggests that the usage draws attention to its essential ingredient.[36]

The choice of *kruptō*[37] (to hide) to describe the woman's action
needs careful attention. Normally one would expect the verb
phuraō (to knead).[38] The figurative usage of hiding to describe
mixing leaven and flour is otherwise unknown in Greek. *Kruptō*
also has negative overtones. In contrast to the more neutral
kaluptō (to cover), *kruptō* emphasizes the subjective element.
According to Albrecht Oepke "the concealment is often for selfish
reasons, e.g., to prevent others from using the object, to keep it
for oneself."[39] New Testament examples of such usage occur in
the parables of the Hidden Treasure (Matt. 13:44) and the Talents
(Matt. 25:18). *Kruptō* definitely connotes negative concealment.

The amount of bread that the woman bakes is also unusual.[40]
Jeremias estimates that three measures at about fifty pounds
would provide enough bread for a hundred people, destroying
the scene's everydayness.[41] A Palestinian audience would have
been tipped off that this was no ordinary baking session. Jeremias points to Gen. 18:6 as a possible background for three
measures. The story deals with Abraham's reception of the three
visitors, one of them the Lord, at the Oaks of Mamre. He
instructs Sarah, "Make ready quickly three measures of fine
meal, knead it, and make cakes." Funk pursues Jeremias's suggestion to two other occasions in the Old Testament where three
measures is used.[42] When the angel of the Lord appears to
Gideon, Gideon prepares for him "a kid, and unleavened cakes
from an ephah of flour" (Judg. 6:19). An ephah of flour is three
measures. Likewise when Hannah takes Samuel to the temple
to dedicate him to the Lord, among the gifts she offers is an
ephah of flour (1 Sam. 1:24). These examples suggest that not
only is three measures more than normal, but also that it is
connected with an epiphany. To hide leaven stands in contrast
with three measures (an epiphany).

Finally, Funk questions the appropriateness of leaven as a symbol for Kingdom.[43] Jeremias had noted that leaven was a symbol for malice and wickedness,[44] but he saw no significance in it. Leaven as a symbol for evil has a long history within Judaism. In the commands for celebrating Passover leavened bread was forbidden. "And you shall observe the feast of the unleavened bread, . . . For seven days no leaven shall be found in your houses; for if any one eats what is leavened, that person shall be cut off from the congregation of Israel, . . ." (Exod. 12:17–20).[45]

In the New Testament, leaven's association with evil is implied in the proverb, "Do you not know that a little leaven leavens the whole lump?" (1 Cor. 5:6; Gal. 5:9). Both times the proverb occurs in a context where the congregation is being reproved for going astray. The point is that just a little bad can ruin all the good.[46] "Cleanse out the old leaven that you may be a new lump, as you really are unleavened" (1 Cor. 5:7). The proverb summarizes the common experience of how easily a little evil can corrupt the whole. Not only does the proverb assume this common-sense story, but leaven alone can stand for the whole story. "Beware of the leaven of the Pharisees" (Mark 8:15). The disciples are led to understand that this refers to the Pharisees' teaching, so that even a little involvement with their teaching will corrupt everything.

In the Old Testament the Prophet Hosea exemplifies the leaven's development into a symbol for moral corruption.

> They are all adulterers;
> they are like a heated oven,
> whose baker ceases to stir the fire,
> from the kneading of the dough
> until it is leavened.
> (Hos. 7:4)

The quote is an important and neglected parallel to our parable. It confirms that the leavening process was a symbol for moral corruption. Furthermore, it highlights the parable's description of the woman hiding leaven: in Hosea dough is kneaded. Finally, the conclusion of the leavening process, "until it is leavened," demonstrates the inevitable conquest of a little evil over every-thing.[47] Thus the parable's conclusion, "until it was all leav-ened," is part of the proverb of leaven.

In the parable three powerful images are set in juxtaposition: leaven, with overtones of moral perversion; hiding, with over-tones of deliberate concealment; and three measures, with its overtones of divine manifestation, epiphany. To compare King-dom to leaven means that Kingdom has an inverse relation to what is normally considered religious.[48] Its manifestation, three measures, is concealed because it is leaven. Its activity will work its way through everything, "till it [is] all leavened." If one takes seriously leaven's significance as represented in Paul's proverb and the quote from Hosea, then Kingdom will work its way through everything as a moral perversion, undermining normal religious perceptions. In this sense it is destructive, subversive and shattering—its own sacramentality is a hidden epiphany.

Kingdom's outcome is clear in the three measures which, as an image for an epiphany, is surely comic (Thesis I). That every-thing is to be leavened reinforces this by ensuring that the Kingdom's activity will reach its completion. The two other im-ages, leaven and hiding, imply tragedy. By using leaven, the parable announces that the sacred's manifestation is an inver-sion of expectation. Likewise, since it is hidden, it can be missed and those who would seek Kingdom risk loss of their normal perception of the sacred because it is under another guise.

To enter the parable places great demands upon the hearer's faith (Thesis V). The parable's selection of images demands faith, for it expresses a new vision of Kingdom. To see leaven as compatible with three measures demands faith on the hearer's part. This parable seeks to orient a hearer toward the identifica-tion of God within everyday experience. God is at work like leaven, that is, he is undermining the everyday, inverting it. The religious tradition as predictive of God's locus can no longer serve to demarcate where he is at work. His work is not obvious, but is like moral perversion among the good. It corrupts what-ever it touches. So it is with Kingdom.

The hearer's faith is severely challenged because the parable articulates such a radical vision of God. It also gives clear expression to the faith of the parable teller. His faith is expressed in the conviction that not only is God at work but that he, the parable teller, can point to that activity. This in turn demands a faith relationship between teller and hearer. The hearer is asked implicitly to trust the teller's vision: is this a description of how God is manifested?

FIG TREE
(Mark 13:28)

The saying now occurs in the context of the apocalyptic discourse of Mark's gospel. The discourse's construction is a problematic question in Marcan studies, but there is general consensus that it is made up of pieces of tradition.[49] The parable stands in the final sequence dealing with the parousia of the Son of Man. Such a parousia theology is a construction of the early community. Bultmann has pointed out that the parable is not a good illustration of its application. "It is a striking fact that the truth which the similitude illustrates is not to be seen in the *humeis* (you), but that the *humeis* (you) are to draw the concluding application."[50] We can therefore conclude that v. 28 is a free-floating logion that has been inserted into the context of the coming of the Son of Man.

This one-liner, like the two previous ones, is deceptive in its simplicity. On the surface it appears to be no more than a folk lesson on the observation of the approach of summer. But it too has its resonances that, if listened to closely, create dissonance.

Fig trees were among the more prominent trees of Palestine and became in the Old Testament a figure for the blessings of the land. In Moses' speech in Deut. 8:7–8, the fig tree appears among the promised land's characteristics. "For the Lord your God is bringing you into a good land, a land of brooks of water, of fountains and springs, flowing forth in valleys and hills, a land of wheat and barley, of vines and fig trees and pomegranates, . . ." In time the list is narrowed down so that vine and fig tree are signs of blessing. "Judah and Israel dwelt in safety, from Dan even to Beersheba, every man under his vine and under his fig tree, all the days of Solomon" (1 Kings 4:25). Conversely, its destruction stands for a curse upon the land. "'I smote you with blight and mildew; I laid waste your gardens and your vine-yards; your fig trees and your olive trees the locust devoured; yet you did not return to me,' says the Lord" (Amos 4:9).

The fig tree's literal presence as a blessing or its literal absence as a curse, allows the fig tree to function as a figure for blessing or curse. For example, in Hos. 9:10 the fig tree is used as an image of God's love for Israel's fathers. "Like grapes in the wilderness, I found Israel. Like the first fruit on the fig tree, in its first season, I saw your fathers." Or in Mic. 4:4 the fig tree is part of the vision of Israel's future blessing associated with the restoration of the Davidic kingdom. "But they shall sit every man under his vine and under his fig tree, and none shall make them afraid; for the mouth of the Lord of hosts has spoken." The fig tree's presence summarizes as proverbial insight man's happiness.

Its bearing or not bearing fruit is likewise a sign of blessing or curse. These figurative possibilities are part of the inherited (dia-chronic) language stock associated with the image. Also, unlike other prominent trees of Palestine, the fig tree is not evergreen but sheds its leaves during winter, "so that the bare spiky twigs which give it an appearance of being utterly dead, make it possible to watch the return of the rising sap with special clearness."[51]

"From the fig tree learn the parable" (au. trans.). Because of the fig tree's associations, this verse was not as puzzling to Jesus' audience as to our ears. The fig tree has figurative value as a sign of blessing. "As soon as its branch becomes tender and puts forth its leaves, you know that summer is near" (Mark 13:28). But the parable does not exploit that symbolic value; it only says that when sap rises in its bare branches you know summer is near.[52] As a symbol for blessedness the expected parable should not be the coming of summer but the future blessedness. As *parable* it should refer to something other than itself. But by turning attention to its naturalness, the parable demythologizes the fig tree's symbolism and returns it to its natural environment. It is a parable in not being a parable.

The parable could be a paradigm for the congruity of the secular and religious in the World of parable (Thesis III). By demythologizing the fig tree, the parable turns attention to the natural as a referent for understanding future blessedness. The fig tree draws attention to the parable's topic: the blessedness of Kingdom. But the parable is not drawn from the fig tree's figurative possibilities, rather from its natural budding.

Like the mustard plant, implicit within the parable is the notion of the Kingdom's miraculous nature. The budding fig tree is not only a figure of God's mercy but also a type of resurrection motif. The image of a fig tree dying in winter is tragic, but the promise of a budding Kingdom is comic (Thesis I). The hearer is thereby forced to reflect upon his everyday experience as the place for the coming Kingdom. It comes not with great apocalyptic signs, but with an approach of summer.

SEED CAST UPON THE GROUND
(Mark 4:26–29)

Because of the role this parable has played in the discussion of Jesus' eschatology, it provides an occasion for considering this debated topic as related to parables. Three interpreters will be examined as representatives of major positions. For Dodd, the parable exemplified realized eschatology; for W. G. Kümmel, its eschatology was both present and future; for Jeremias, the eschatological interpretation is related to Jesus' defense of his preaching of the Kingdom. Each in turn exposes a decisive methodological question.

Dodd devotes considerable attention to the parable as an archetype of what he called "the parables of growth."[53] For him, a principal problem facing an interpreter concerns determining "whether the Kingdom of God is like the seed, or like what happens when seed is sown: whether it is like the growth or like the harvest."[54] He describes three traditional interpretations dependent upon one point of the comparison. If seed is the point of comparison, then the Kingdom is an interior principle: "The kingdom of God is within you."[55] A second group interprets the parable in an evolutionary fashion, the growth of the seed being the point of the parable. Finally, the eschatological interpretation, identified with Albert Schweitzer, sees the point of comparison in the harvest. Jesus himself is the Harvester and "when, very shortly, the Kingdom of God comes . . . He is revealed in glory."[56] While finding fault with each of these positions, Dodd maintains that methodologically, "the interpretation of the parables depends upon the view taken of the Kingdom of God."[57] Thus an understanding of Kingdom is not dependent upon parable, but the parable's interpretation is dependent upon a prior understanding of Kingdom.

In Dodd's view the Kingdom is neither an evolutionary process nor a catastrophic event in the future, "but a present crisis."[58] With this framework, Dodd turns to the parable. The harvest is a symbol for the Day of the Lord, or Day of Judgment,[59] and he refers to Matt. 9:37–38//Luke 10:2, where Jesus calls for the Lord of the Harvest to send laborers. This saying is the key for Dodd: now is the harvest and Jesus is putting in the sickle.[60] The difference between Dodd and Schweitzer ultimately revolves around the time of the harvest, and that time is determined not from the parable, but from outside.

Dodd's study shows the importance of a theory of metaphor for interpreting a parable. He is correct that the problem in the history of interpretation revolves around determining which "point" of the parable is comparable to the Kingdom. But instead of seeing the entire parable as a metaphor for Kingdom, he sees the parable as a narrow simile. Likewise, as Dodd admits, the "point" cannot be determined by the parable, but one must look outside. In the final analysis Dodd commits the parable to allegory, albeit an eschatological one. Even though he is identified in the history of scholarship with realized eschatology, he remains fixed upon understanding eschatology as chronological time.

The interpretations of Kümmel and Jeremias further illustrate the problems set forth by Dodd. Both interpreters are in conscious disagreement with Dodd, and yet they remain trapped by his questions.

Kümmel displays a remarkable degree of agreement with Dodd. He agrees that the question facing the exegete has to do with "which features are to be compared with the Kingdom of God."[61] Also, since the end of the parable alludes to Joel 3:13, the harvest represents eschatological judgment. Further, he rejects a developmental, evolutionary understanding of Kingdom. Because the farmer has no part in the growth of the seed, the harvest comes without his aid. This for Kümmel is the point of the parable: "not the growth of the crop, but the certain arrival of the harvest which nothing can influence."[62]

Because Kümmel's interpretation is very close to Dodd's, he argues that the harvest does not refer to a present crisis. If it did, the parable would only be a summons and "would also contain the idea of a development of the kingdom of God from the time of the prophets to that of Jesus, an idea which radically contradicts Matt. 11:12."[63] For Kümmel it has a comforting purpose: "The kingdom of God comes surely without our being able to hinder or to hasten it; the secrecy of its present reality must not be allowed to endanger this certainty."[64] The point is not the harvest but the secret growing. He interprets it as a timetable: while Kingdom is already secretly here in the sowing, one is still to await its future harvest. Despite his rejection of a theory of development, he has fallen victim to such a theory. His interpretation, like Dodd's, remains tied to his theory of Kingdom and thus the parable is the Kingdom's allegory.

Jeremias agrees that in this parable the advent of the Kingdom is compared to a harvest; the harvest is a reference to Joel 3:13 and refers to the Last Judgment. But Jeremias avoids the timetable approach to the parable and instead relates the parable to an explicit controversy between Jesus and the zealots. The farmer's inability to make his crops grow is Jesus' response to the question of action.

> Why did Jesus not act when action was what the hour demanded? Why did he not take vigorous steps to purge out the sinners and establish the purified community . . . ? Why did he not give the signal for the liberation of Israel from the Gentile yoke . . . ? Was not this refusal of Jesus a denial of the claim of his mission?[65]

Jesus' response is the parable: patience is man's response.

The strength of Jeremias's interpretation is that he comes very close to considering the parable as whole and does not decide upon one single allegorical point. But his weakness is that he is both dependent upon a prior understanding of the mission of Jesus and also upon a tentative situation of debate with zealots. For Jeremias, the parable's point is that Kingdom grows by itself (*automatē*).

The survey corroborates the validity of our original starting point, namely, the importance of parables as guide to Jesus' understanding of Kingdom. These three examples indicate the futility of using a predetermined understanding of Kingdom as a key for interpreting a parable. This imposes silence upon parable, since it is not allowed to speak but is manipulated to confirm a point or position. Because the interpretation comes from outside the parable, there are no criteria within a parable for judging an interpretation.

If progress is to be made, then the parable as whole, not some part, must be seen as the metaphor for Kingdom. This means that first we must examine the Marcan context for any clues it may contain, expose the parable's structure, and finally listen for diachronic resonances.

One striking problem concerning this parable's place in Mark is its omission from Matthew and Luke.[66] Arguments from silence are usually problematic, but why did the other synoptics choose not to use the parable? Was the parable unintelligible to them? Or was it so insignificant that they could find no use for it? While we may never know, the omission from Matthew and Luke does suggest that the parable may be more mysterious than first guessed.

Because the construction of Mark 4 has been a debated topic in recent research, we need to ask whether the parable has undergone significant redactional reworking. No one doubts the chapter's importance in the overall Marcan redaction. It is only one of two major speeches given by Jesus (the other is chapter 13). But the organization of material inherited by Mark is controversial. Theodore Weeden in his study maintained that the Mustard Seed and the Seed Cast upon the Ground were joined by Mark's opponents with the Sower and its interpretation, prior to Mark's redaction, to support a *theios aner* theology.[67] Heinz-Wolfgang Kuhn also argued for a pre-Marcan collection held together by the key words "sower," "seed," and "sowing" and the pre-Marcan attachment formula, *kai elegen.*[68]

On the other hand, Werner Kelber has challenged the pre-Marcan collection, maintaining that Mark himself is responsible for the chapter's present arrangement.[69] Important for our consideration is Kelber's argument that the Seed Cast upon the

Ground was not originally a Kingdom parable. He states that the formula *kai elegen* need not be pre-Marcan,[70] and suggests that possibly neither the Seed Cast upon the Ground nor the Mustard Seed were originally Kingdom parables.[71] The clumsiness of the introduction to the parable indicates for Kelber that the theme of Kingdom has been added to the parables.[72]

The arguments are of unequal weight. Whether or not there was a pre-Marcan collection of parables does not affect the parable's interpretation at the level of our concern.[73] But the second argument is more serious. Does the clumsiness of the introduction in Greek suggest redactional seaming or translation? Jeremias has argued that the Greek represents an attempt to translate an Aramaic comparison formula.[74] Furthermore, if Mark is to be given credit as an author of great skill, why are his seams clumsy and inadequate? On the whole, I find Jeremias's argument sounder in that he explains the text on the basis of known factors, whereas Kelber's argument is based on suggestions.

One element, however, appears to result from redaction. The conclusion reads, "immediately he puts in the sickle, for the harvest has come." The suspect word is "immediately" (*euthus*), a favorite Marcan word.[75] Furthermore, such a usage would cohere with the redactional intention as seen in Mark 1:15, where the at-handness of the Kingdom is stressed. For these reasons one should be careful about basing an understanding of the parable upon the word.[76]

Having arrived at an established text, we now turn our attention to the structure of the parable. At first glance there is some question as to whether it should be classified as a one-liner or a narrative. Two factors tell in favor of its being a one-liner. First is the subjunctive, conditional character of the parable. According to Blass and Debrunner, conditional relative clauses "usually make no assertions about concrete realities, but rather general assertions or suppositions."[77] They list as analogous to Mark 4:26 three Septuagint texts, from Isa. 7:2; 17:11; 31:4.[78] In each case the comparison is drawn from some inevitable fact of nature. The consistent use of the subjunctive in the parable shows that this is not an indicative narrative but a general description of a recurring phenomenon.

Similarly, the parable's careful structuring prevents a single subject from emerging, a figure around which narrative action could be organized. Rather the parable has a careful stair-step organization.

(1)   A man / should cast / *seed* / upon the **ground**

(2)   — / should sleep and should rise up

(3)   *seed* / should sprout and grow
      (as he does not know)

(4)   (by itself) the **ground** / fruit-produces
      (a) first grass
      (b) then an ear
      (c) then the full seed in the ear

(5)   and when [it] is ready / the fruit

This schema reveals several elements normally missed in an English translation. The nouns of line 1 each in turn become the subject of the next three clauses, again pointing out that there is no single unifying subject to the parable. There are two verbs each in lines 2 and 3. The verb of line 4 is a compound word in Greek, *karpophoreo* (to bear fruit), and its noun component *karpos* (fruit) is the subject of the next verb *paradoi* (ready). Lines 3 and 4 have a chiastic structure, as indicated by the phrases in parentheses. This ties the two lines together and reinforces the man's passivity. Finally, the desciption of growth in 4a, 4b, and 4c, mirrors the threefold pattern of lines 1, 2, and 3.

Attention to the structure indicates a deliberate delaying tactic on the parable's part. The stair-step pattern and the elaborate description of what the ground brings forth reinforce this. Both the careful structuring and the elongation of line 4 indicate that the hearer of the parable would retain the whole picture as the "point" of the parable.

Since this is a one-liner like the others, it presumes a common story. We must now discover that common, traditional story. The presiding image of the parable is the agricultural process itself, and since the parable as *mashal* is part of Israel's wisdom tradition, the images of the parable should reflect that tradition.

The audience conjures up certain images when in the first line the man casts seed upon the ground. A planting/harvest motif is common in wisdom literature. Ps. 126:5–6 contrasts the two. "May those who sow in tears reap with shouts of joy!" The obvious labor of planting, contrasted with harvest's joy and gratification, becomes the implied story for a proverb: "The sluggard does not plow in the autumn; he will seek at harvest and have nothing" (Prov. 20:4). Or the proverbs can be reversed: "A son who gathers in summer is prudent, but a son who sleeps in harvest brings shame" (Prov. 10:5). In Hos. 10:11–12, the proverb can be used to encourage Israel to return to the Lord. "Sow for yourselves righteousness, reap the fruit of steadfast love; . . . for it is the time to seek the Lord, that he may come and rain salvation upon you."[79] In Isa. 28:24 the regularity of the farmer's activity is used as an example of how the Lord instructs his people.

> Does he who plows for sowing plow continually?
>   does he continually open and harrow his ground?
> When he has leveled its surface,
>   does he not scatter dill, sow cummin,
> and put in wheat in rows
>   and barley in its proper place,
>   and spelt as the border?

This text also illustrates the steps from sowing to harvest. In contrast, our parable limits the farmer's activity to one line, and the seed receives the balance of attention. This should alert us to a dissonance in the parable, a jarring of the everyday. Since the proverbial story implies that the act of planting foresees harvesting (e.g., Prov. 20:4), the audience assumes that the casting of the seed foretells the end. As a metaphor for Kingdom, the parable's description somehow images Kingdom, but the constant changing of subject prevents the audience from fixing upon a single subject. The man's passivity, his ignorance of what is going on, and the missing description of normal activity after sowing suggests that he is a sluggard. Therefore, the harvest is in doubt.

A second element in the parable reflects the audience's tradition. In line 4 the parable says, "by itself the ground produces fruit." "By itself" translates the Greek adjective *automatos*, which is used of things that have no visible cause, and therefore has about it a sense of the mysterious. For example, it describes doors opening by themselves; cf. Acts 12:10.[80] In the Septuagint it is used to translate the Hebrew *sapiyah*, which is "what springs up of itself in the second year, and served as food when no grain could be sown."[81] It is used in Lev. 25:5 (and 11) in the command for the seventh year rest.

> Six years you shall sow your field . . . but in the seventh year there shall be a sabbath of solemn rest for the land, a sabbath to the Lord, you shall not sow your field . . . . What grows *by itself* (LXX *automata*) in your harvest you shall not reap.[82]

The fruit that grows of itself is also used to signal God's grace in Isa. 37:30, a proof of his caring for his people.

> "And this shall be the sign for you: this year eat what grows of itself, and in the second year what springs of the same; then in the third year sow and reap, . . ."

In the parable *automatos*, a Greek translation for the Hebrew technical term for produce that "grows of itself," interacts with the man's passivity. The allusion sounds a resonance within the text, alerting the audience to the grace of God present in the land on sabbatical. The allusion is not meant literally, but as a metaphorical reference to the graced character of the land.

Finally, in the last line of the parable commentators have seen a reference to Joel 3:13. The context of Joel 3:13 provides important clues for understanding the reference.

> (9) Proclaim this among the nations:
> Prepare war, . . .
> (10) Beat your plowshares into swords,
> and your pruning forks into spears; . . .
> (12) Let the nations . . . come up to the valley of Jehoshaphat; for there I will sit to judge
> all the nations round about.
> (13) Put in the sickle,
> for the harvest is ripe.

>   Go in, tread,
>   for the wine press is full.
>   The vats overflow,
>   for their wickedness is great. . . .
>   (14) For the day of the Lord is near.

The parable's allusion to Joel 3:13 raises a critical problem. Jeremias and others[83] argue that the context in Joel indicates that the harvest is to be equated with Last Judgment. While the harvest motif is used in Joel for Judgment, is it so used in the parable? The context is decidedly different in Joel and the parable. Joel's context is the final eschatological war. In v. 10 the reversal of Isa. 2:4 and Mic. 4:3 indicates the boldness of his metaphor. To allude to Joel, with its context, is to fix the harvest in very definite terms. But the parable's context is the opposite. As we saw above, the careful structuring of the parable indicates passivity, a careful delaying. The man's ignorance about how the crop grows, his lack of further effort, his sleeping and rising day and night and the peaceful sabbatical of the land contrast the parable with Joel. The allusion in the final line to Joel suggests that the hearer has been lulled into a trap.[84] The audience fell asleep waiting for the eschatological war.

We began with a discussion of the parable's importance for an understanding of Jesus' eschatology. But for the parable to decide the Kingdom's presence or futurity, two things were necessary: First, a prior understanding of Kingdom must be derived from outside the parable, and second, the point must be identified with harvest. But as we have implied, harvest in the parable is not an allegorial timetable for the Last Judgment. From the parable's viewpoint,[85] the question of eschatology in terms of *chronos*, chronological arrival, presence, or futurity, is a question so poorly framed as to be unanswerable.

There is in this parable an eschatology of reversal, but it has the character of grace. Our third thesis concerning grace states that grace comes to those who have no alternative. In this parable, grace as eschatology is *kairos*, not *chronos*. The images of sowing/reaping and the land on sabbatical are so dissonant with the harvest as eschatological war that they refract a new context for the harvest, radically different as image from that of Joel. This juxtaposition of images creates a new metaphor which in turn refracts the symbol Kingdom of God. The new metaphor exposes the experience of Yahweh as King. In this sense, Kingdom comes as *kairos*; it does not come at a particular *chronos*. For the one who can accept Kingdom on the parable's terms, *kairos* is a moment of grace; having begun with sowing, harvest comes not as apocalyptic war, but the inevitable result of planting. What will be reaped is what is sown.

The parable's construction forces the hearer to make a decision about the type of harvest. Is harvest to be characterized by its original context in Joel or by the new terms dictated by the parable? That the parable forces this decision is evident from the assumed story of the *mashal*. The sowing/reaping theme assumes that what is sown is what will be reaped. The hearer is forced to decide what context to supply for the harvest, thereby giving it meaning. To abandon Joel's description and its implied apocalyptic ideology[86] renders the hearer dependent upon the parable's depiction of World. It is to place one's faith in that World as metaphorically created and to trust the parable teller's ability to perceive correctly the outlines of reality (Thesis V). It likewise demands an ability to see that Kingdom can be depicted adequately by the simple description of farm life. The language may resonate deep within the tradition, but on the surface it still remains the story of a farmer's day-after-day existence. Of such is Kingdom. To place faith in so ordinary a phenomenon as Kingdom is to abandon the faith of old and to seek after another.

NOTES

1. In chap. 2 the problems associated with trying to specify the differences between differing types of *meshalim* were discussed. Adolf Jülicher treats the distinction between similitude and parable in *Die Gleichnisreden Jesu* (Darmstadt: Wissenschaftliche Buchgesellschaft, 1969; first published 1899–1910), 1:80ff., 88ff. The identification of parable with narrative has become a tendency in some recent criticism. The most recent example is John Dominic Crossan in *Cliffs of*

Fall: Paradox and Polyvalence in the Parables of Jesus (New York: Seabury Press, 1980), chap. 1, where parable is defined as short, narrative paradoxes. This tendency divorces parable from the form *mashal*.

2. Rudolf Bultmann, *History of the Synoptic Tradition*, hereinafter *HST*, trans. John Marsh (New York: Harper and Row, 1963), p. 174; C. H. Dodd, *The Parables of the Kingdom* (New York: Charles Scribner's Sons, 1961), p. 7, "It cannot be pretended that the line can be drawn with any precision between these three classes of parable." Jeremias is silent on the types of parables. There are some classifications in Jeremias, but he does not deal with them in a systematic fashion, e.g., double-edged parables (*Parables*, p. 38), or again "The parables about the goodness . . . were addressed without exception to opponents and critics" (p. 65).

3. Joachim Jeremias, *The Parables of Jesus*, trans. H. S. Hooke (New York: Charles Scribner's Sons, 1963), p. 101.

4. Ibid.

5. *Early Christian Rhetoric: The Language of the Gospel* (Cambridge: Harvard University Press, 1st ed., 1964), p. 80.

6. Robert Funk, *Language, Hermeneutic and the Word of God* (New York: Harper and Row, 1966), p. 147.

7. *HST*, p. 175.

8. *Parables of the Kingdom*, p. 5.

9. "Uses of the Proverbs in the Synoptic Gospels," *Interpretation* 24 (1970): 61–76; "The Proverb," *Literary Criticism of the New Testament*, Guides to Biblical Scholarship (Philadelphia: Fortress Press, 1970), pp. 30–41.

10. "The Proverb," p. 34.

11. "Uses of Proverbs," pp. 65–66. In this essay Beardslee understands parable as narrative parable.

12. Ibid., p. 65.

13. Ibid., p. 66. Beardslee does not use insight in the technical sense of Bernard Lonergan. However, his usage appears to me to be compatible with Lonergan's. Proverb is an instance of what Lonergan calls insight.

14. Ibid., p. 67.

15. E.g., "Whoever loses his life will preserve it" (Luke 17:33); "Love your enemies, do good to those who hate you" (Luke 6:27).

16. Ibid.

17. Ibid., p. 69.

18. John Dominic Crossan, *In Parables* (New York: Harper and Row, 1973), pp. 45ff.

19. Ibid., p. 46. Crossan is dependent upon the observations of

John R. Donahue, *Are You the Christ?* (Missoula: SBL Dissertation Series, 1973), pp. 58ff.

20. Ibid.

21. The conflation of Mark and Q is seen in that the shrub (Mark) grows into a tree (Luke/Q); cf., Bultmann, *HST*, p. 172.

22. Crossan, *In Parables*, p. 48.

23. Walter Bauer, *A Greek-English Lexicon of the New Testament*, hereinafter *BAG*, trans. William Arndt and Wilbur Gingrich, 2d rev. ed. by Gingrich and Frederick W. Danker (Chicago: University of Chicago Press, 1979), p. 753.

24. *In Parables*, p. 49. Crossan has been misled at this point because of his rejection of any reference to the "apocalyptic tree," cf., below.

25. I have assumed that Thomas did not know the synoptics. If he did, the reference would be derived from Mark or Matthew. Although the question of the relation of Thomas to the synoptics is debated, the argument from order by B. de Solages, "L'Évangile de Thomas et les Évangiles canoniques: l'ordre des péricopes," *Bulletin de littérature ecclésiastique* 80 (1979): 102–8, seems clearly to indicate non-dependence.

26. *In Parables*, pp. 47ff.

27. Ibid., p. 48. As will become evident, this is exactly what Jesus intended. Funk, *Jesus as Precursor*, Semeia Studies (Philadelphia: Fortress Press; Missoula: Scholars Press, 1975), pp. 20ff., assumes too easily the reference to Ezekiel.

28. *In Parables*, p. 50. The model for the Great Tree was the Cedar of Lebanon.

29. Ernst Käsemann, "On Paul's Anthropology," *Perspectives on Paul*, trans. Margaret Kohl (Philadelphia: Fortress Press, 1971), pp. 8ff., develops the theme of God's miracle associated with the analogy of growth.

30. Funk, *Jesus as Precursor*, pp. 22–23, shows that even in the interpretation of Dodd and Jeremias the expectation of the Great Tree has continued to triumph.

31. Funk, ibid., while ignoring the element of miracle, accents the burlesque of Israel's expectation.

32. *Parables of Jesus*, p. 149. Dodd, *Parables of the Kingdom*, p. 155, takes it as an example of how the ministry "swelled and bubbled like fermentation."

33. Jeremias, *Parables of Jesus*, p. 146. Dodd sees both as parables of growth, but attempts to separate their interpretation. Recently,

J. Lambreck, *Parables of Jesus*, trans. Rene Van de Walle and Christopher Begg (Bangalore, India: Theological Publications in India, 1976), p. 152, despite careful redactional study, still sees the two parables as "twins."

34. *Jesus as Precursor*, p. 59. The translation of the *New American Bible* scrubs the parable so clean that it is no longer a parable: "The reign of God is like yeast which a woman took and kneaded into three measures of flour. Eventually the whole mass of dough began to rise."

35. *Parables of the Kingdom*, p. 155.

36. *Jesus as Precursor*, p. 60.

37. Matthew has used *egkruptō*, which does not affect this meaning.

38. The noun form, *phurama* (lump), occurs five times in the New Testament: 1 Cor. 5:6; Gal. 5:9; Rom. 9:21, 11:16.

39. *"Kruptō," Theological Dictionary of the New Testament*, ed. Gerhard Kittel, trans. Geoffrey Bromiley (Grand Rapids: Eerdmans, 1968), 3:958ff.

40. Funk, *Jesus as Precursor*, p. 50, observes this point.

41. *Parables of Jesus*, p. 147.

42. *Jesus as Precursor*, pp. 60–62.

43. Ibid., pp. 62–63.

44. *Parables of Jesus*, p. 149. H. L. Strack and P. Billerbeck, *Kommentar zum Neuen Testamentum aus Talmud und Midrasch* (Munich: C. H. Beck, 1926) at Matt. 16:6 quotes rabbinic evidence for the negative character of leaven.

45. Cf. also, Exod. 34:25; Lev. 2:11, 6:17, 10:12.

46. A modern equivalent is "one rotten apple spoils the whole barrel."

47. The LXX is remarkably close to the end of the parable, "until it is leavened" (*heōs tou zumōthēnai auto*). In fact, these two texts are so similar that they surely belong to the same trajectory.

48. E.g., at Hos. 7:4 substitute "Kingdom" for "adulterers."

49. Rudolf Pesch, *Naherwartungen* (Düsseldorf: Patmos-Verlag, 1968); Willi Marxsen, *Mark the Evangelist*, trans. Roy A. Harrisville (Nashville: Abingdon Press, 1969), pp. 151–206. For a recent redactional interpretation of Mark 13 see Werner Kelber, *The Kingdom in Mark* (Philadelphia: Fortress Press, 1974), chap. 6.

50. *HST*, p. 173; likewise Jeremias, *Parables of Jesus*, p. 119.

51. Jeremias, *Parables of Jesus*, p. 120.

52. Contra Jeremias, ibid., the parable makes no mention of resurrection; in fact it avoids allegorical reference.

53. *Parables of the Kingdom*, chap. 6. This group includes for

Dodd, the Sower, the Tares, the Seed Growing Secretly, the Mustard Seed, the Leaven, and the Drag-net. Nils Dahl, "The Parables of Growth," *Studia Theologica*, 5 (1951): 132–66, developed Dodd's category in a seminal study of the eschatology of Jesus. See my "Parables of Growth Revisited," *Biblical Theology Bulletin* 11 (1981), pp. 3–9.

54. Dodd, ibid., p. 141; likewise W. G. Kümmel: "The picture itself is completely plain and in its exegesis we have only to inquire which features are to be compared with the Kingdom of God" (*Promise and Fulfillment*, trans. Dorothea M. Barton, Studies in Biblical Theology 23 [London, SCM Press, 1957], p. 128); Jeremias, *Parables of Jesus*, p. 151, assumes the point of comparison is the harvest.

55. Ibid., p. 141. Although Dodd does not identify an interpreter by name, this is typical of Protestant liberalism at the turn of the century. The text quoted, Luke 17:21, was a favorite of Adolf von Harnack.

56. Ibid., p. 142.

57. Ibid.; the opposite view is taken in this book.

58. Ibid., p. 143.

59. Ibid. Dodd refers to Joel 3:13, which is alluded to in the parable's last line.

60. Ibid., pp. 143–44.

61. *Promise and Fulfillment*, p. 128.

62. Ibid.

63. Ibid., p. 129.

64. Ibid.

65. *Parables of Jesus*, p. 152.

66. This omission is a problem for William Farmer, *The Synoptic Problem* (New York: Macmillan Company, 1964), p. 212. For Farmer the fact that Mark can be reconstructed from Matthew and Luke proves Marcan dependence, not priority. The other omitted material is Mark 7:32–35; 8:22–26.

67. *Mark—Traditions in Conflict* (Philadelphia: Fortress Press, 1971), p. 147.

68. *Ältere Sammlungen im Markusevangelium*, Studien zur Umwelt des Neuen Testaments 8 (Göttingen: Vandenhoeck und Ruprecht, 1971): 99–146.

69. *The Kingdom in Mark* (Philadelphia: Fortress Press, 1974), pp. 29–30. For Kelber the parable of the sower and its interpretation were joined prior to Mark, but the rest are "redactional accretions."

70. Ibid., p. 30; Kelber is indebted to the study of Maximilian Zerwick, *Untersuchungen zum Markus-Stil: Ein Beitrag zur stilistischen Durcharbeitung des Neuen Testaments* (Rome: Pontifical Biblical In-

stitute, 1937), p. 8. Zerwick argued tentatively that the formula could be Marcan. Paul Achtemeier, *Mark*, Proclamation Commentaries (Philadelphia: Fortress Press, 1975), p. 66, agrees that *kai elegen* is a variation of the Marcan connective formula and sees the arrangement of chap. 4 as Marcan. He does not argue that the Kingdom introduction formula is Marcan.

71. Ibid., p. 29.

72. It is interesting to note in Kelber's argument that what is tentative and suggestive becomes established fact at the end of the argument (ibid., p. 30).

73. The appearance of the Mustard Seed in Q as a Kingdom parable indicates that the Kingdom motif was part of the tradition, not a Marcan creation.

74. Jeremias, *Parables of Jesus*, p. 101.

75. The word occurs forty-two times in Mark; seven in Matthew; once in Luke. Crossan, *In Parables*, pp. 84–85, without evidence sees v. 28 as an addition.

76. Jeremias, *Parables of Jesus*, p. 151, implies that the *euthus* serves to contrast the passivity of the farmer after planting with the sudden activity of the harvest.

77. A *Greek Grammar of the New Testament*, trans. Robert Funk (Chicago: University of Chicago Press, 1961), no. 380.

78. Ibid., no. 380(4).

79. Cf., the similar motif in Isa. 9:3; Ezek. 36:8–10; Job 4:8–9; Hos. 6:11; Amos 9:13; conversely a lack of harvest can stand as a sign of rejection, Joel 1:11; Isa. 16:10, 17:11.

80. *BAG*, p. 122.

81. Brown, Driver, Briggs, A *Hebrew and English Lexicon of the Old Testament* (Oxford: Clarendon Press, 1907), p. 705.

82. Marcus Jastrow, A *Dictionary of the Targumin* (New York: Padres Publishing House, 1950), 2:1013, quotes evidence for the continued technical use of the term, even a rabbinical debate concerning the wages of those who watch the after-growth in a Sabbatical year.

83. *Parables of Jesus*, p. 152; Kümmel, *Promise and Fulfillment*, p. 128; Dodd, *Parables of the Kingdom*, p. 143.

84. The structure and performance of this parable is much like that of the Mustard Seed, in which the final line contains an allusion to the Great Tree tradition.

85. I believe this is true of all the so-called parables of Growth.

86. One also would want to agree with Jeremias that the zealot ideology must be abandoned, *Parables of Jesus*, p. 152.

4

TOWARD A GRAMMAR
OF PARABLES

Parables form a gateway to the symbol Kingdom of God. Because of our conviction that a tensive understanding of it is
available through parables, eight parables have been probed in
order to develop insight into Kingdom. But a reader might question whether insight has resulted—has not our analysis led only
to a study of parables, and not to greater precision concerning
Kingdom? Such a question calls attention to the expected end of
parable study. Since parables as metaphors cannot be reduced to
discursive language without loss, how can they provide an insight
into Kingdom?

The quest for a more precise insight requires clarification of
what is meant by insight. Such an effort will provide valuable
clues for our direction. Insight as a methodology entails respond-
ing to parables not simply as particulars, but as a group. This
will lead to the development of abstract, formal models, encom-
passing parables both as particulars and as corpus.

PARABLE AS INSIGHT

Parable, a tensive metaphor, modifies and is modified by a tensive symbol, Kingdom of God. This creates a density of referents, thereby overloading language and compelling insight.[1] As
metaphor, parable insists that A is B, that this is Kingdom—in
metaphor. The form demands an "Ah," an insight on the part
of the hearer. Just as Archimedes ran from the baths of Syracuse
crying "Eureka!" so a hearer of parable receives a sudden illu-
mination when grasping that parable is Kingdom of God. The
hearer's insight is an aperture onto Kingdom from parable.

In parable and Kingdom's intersection, we can distinguish two moments of insight. A particular parable results from and is a manifestation of Jesus' insight into Kingdom as symbol.[2] From all the possible ways in which the symbol could be represented, he has constructed this parable. A second moment of insight occurs when a hearer perceives a parable as metaphor. The parable as aesthetic object creates insight by patterning experience. Art organizes and patterns selections of life so as to concentrate attention. Such concentration is what creates insight, by presenting our imagination a new arrangement of discrete data. This is why art is frequently larger than reality—patterns of experience have been organized so as to make a new experience of reality possible. As Bernard Lonergan says, "It [insight] is truer than experience, leaner, more effective, more to the point."[3]

Artistic insight is verified in the presentation of patterned experience by the work of art. "The artist establishes his insights, not by proof or verification, but by skillfully embodying them in colours and shapes, in sounds and movements, in unfolding situations and actions of fiction."[4] A parable verifies itself. We cannot look behind it for other credentials. For this reason Jesus steadfastly refused to give signs.[5] Parables are their own signs. Their patterning of experience validates in metaphor what they stand for.

An author's patterning of experience indicates intentionality on his part and signals the importance of images in representing insight. Thus parables as metaphors refer to something else or, as insight, they have an intentionality. Such an intentionality results in selecting a particular set of patterned experience. The resulting images enable a hearer to share in the author's insight. This is the intentionality of the speaker—to allow the hearer to participate in the original insight.

Images are necessary to facilitate insight. They derive from concrete, everyday experience. In the example of Archimedes' insight, concrete images of crown, water, floating in the bath, etc., were all necessary to generate his original insight. But insight is not images, nor arranging images into patterned experience; it is a grasping of the relation of the images to the problem's solution. For Lonergan, insight is the grasping.[6] For

Archimedes, the grasping generates not only a solution to his immediate problem but also *universalizes* the images' particularity. Images that generate insight imply a theoretic construction, i.e., they are related to abstract formulations that transcend the particular situation.

The abstract for Lonergan is knowable only through the concrete, which explains the need for images, and is implied in it. Insight is grasping the relation between abstract and concrete.[7] Lonergan shows this in the Archimedes incident. When commissioned to determine whether King Hero's new crown was made of pure gold, Archimedes had an insight into the solution of his problem while taking a bath. His solution was concrete: weigh the crown in water. But to explain why the concrete solution works, one will have recourse to the abstract principles of displacement. Without that abstract point, the weighing of Hero's crown would have no scientific importance.[8] Lonergan concludes that insights "possess a significance greater than their origins and a relevance wider than their original applications."[9] Insight, then, pivots between concrete and abstract.

Lonergan's examples of insight are unfortunately overly scientific, and one might balk at suggesting that this understanding of insight is applicable to parables. And yet with modifications, I believe Lonergan's study can be quite useful. The pivotal character of insight recalls art's universality. Certain works of art may transcend culture and particularity by making a universal claim. This universality is equivalent to what Lonergan calls abstract. Scientific insight leads to abstract theory; art leads to insight into existence itself.

Parables as insight are not exactly parallel to Archimedes' concrete experience and the resulting mathematical formulas. Parables are both the result and generator of insight. They represent Jesus' selection from discrete, concrete data of patterns of experience that generate for a hearer insight into Kingdom.

Because parables re-present selected, organized, patterned experience, they achieve their patterns on the basis of some principle or principles of selection and combination. Such principle or principles ultimately lie within the author's insight and cannot be articulated beyond a mere hint.[10] But the difficulties should not prevent us from attempting a formulation. We must remember that we can never create an abstract model that replaces the original. What we are attempting is to formalize with models the underlying principles of selection and combination that generated the consistent patterning.

How do we go about discovering clues to an underlying structure of parables? I suggest that we appropriate as an analogical guide language itself. Because parables are linguistic phenomena, language as a model is suggestive.[11] Ferdinand de Saussure in his *Course in General Linguistics*[12] distinguishes between *parole* and *langue*. *Parole* indicates a speech act whereas *langue* is equivalent to what we would term language, as in the phrase "English language," a linguistic system. Using this analogy individual parables can be viewed as *parole*, sentences or performances that are governed by underlying rules of grammar, *langue*.[13] Our task is formalizing that underlying grammar. But just as grammatical construction is not equivalent to an individual performance, so the formal models that we will propose cannot substitute for parables themselves.

To develop a parabolic grammar our method will be by necessity both deductive and abstract. Deductive because from the eight parables examined we will deduce a single grammar. This will involve increasing abstraction as we move toward greater generalization, searching for patterns and relations that will encompass the specificity of individual parables. The five theses explored in chapters 2 and 3 have already led to a discursive form of generalization, and now they will guide our formalization process.

Our analysis of parables uncovered two basic types, narrative and one-liner. Analogically, these are two different kinds of sentences or performances. We will first examine the two types of sentences separately to arrive at a grammar for each.

NARRATIVE PARABLES

Narrative parables share in common the obvious fact of narrativity. Is there an order or pattern in the narratives resulting from insight's patterning of experience? To discover this we need a model to illustrate such patterning in an abstract form.

One model proposed for narrative structure is the actantial model.[14] It is a way of abstractly arranging a narrative. The model is as follows:

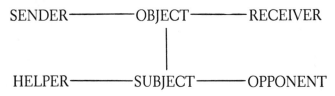

SENDER————————OBJECT————————RECEIVER

HELPER————————SUBJECT————————OPPONENT

A. J. Greimas originally proposed this model as a way of formalizing recurring features of folk tales. Six actants are organized into a series of mutual relations or axes. Actants (the terms in capital letters) are not simply characters, but represent structural constants, functions, roles, etc. Furthermore, three axes or mutual interrelations can be identified. The axis of communication involves the SENDER–OBJECT–RECEIVER line in which a SENDER communicates an OBJECT to a RECEIVER, e.g., a king gives his daughter's hand in matrimony to a prince. The axis of violation relates the SUBJECT–OBJECT. According to Daniel Patte, it can also be termed the axis of plot.[15] In our example, a simple form of this axis would be the prince's search for the princess. On the final axis the subject engages in a test, trial, or ordeal. This series of relations concerns the HELPER–SUBJECT–OPPONENT. Again, the prince, as SUBJECT, must slay the OPPONENT (dragon) by means of the magical spell provided him by the HELPER (wizard).

In actual use not all the model actants need be present in every story, just as in a sentence diagram not every part of speech must be present in every sentence. *The model represents the potentiality of a performance*; a specific performance actualizes and selects only a part of the potentiality.

We aim by this abstract model to uncover a consistent pattern in the actualization (performance) of the narrative parables. The following consistent pattern will emerge: at least one actant is always moved away from an *expected* position in the model to an *unexpected* position. This is a transformational rule of actants for narrative parables. The movement, usually along the axis of power, is dictated by the relation between the comic and the tragic, as isolated in our previous analysis of parables. That is, the thesis that the comic appears under the guise of tragedy dictates, in the story's narrative arrangement, motion from expected to unexpected position.[16] This will become evident in applying the actantial model to each narrative parable.

A. Jerusalem to Jericho (Luke 10:30–35)

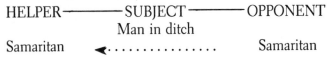

HELPER————— SUBJECT ————— OPPONENT
                Man in ditch
Samaritan   ◄ · · · · · · · · · · · · · · ·   Samaritan

The audience expects the investment[17] of the Samaritan in the actant OPPONENT. But the narative functions as parable only when he is in the position of HELPER. In the text the Samaritan is introduced with an elaborate delaying process that teases the audience.[18] This reinforces the parable's scandal, namely, a Samaritan is HELPER–hero to victim Jew. The comic appears under the guise of tragedy by means of the Samaritan's motion along the axis of power from expected OPPONENT to actual HELPER.

B. A Great Banquet (Luke 14:15–24)

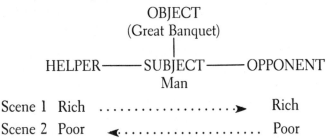

OBJECT
(Great Banquet)
|
HELPER——— SUBJECT ——— OPPONENT
                Man

Scene 1 Rich · · · · · · · · · · · · · · · · · · ·➤   Rich
Scene 2 Poor ◄· · · · · · · · · · · · · · · · · · ·   Poor

The parable's two scenes provide mirror-image investments of the model. For a great banquet the expected HELPERS are the rich, while OPPONENTS are the poor. On this assumption the host makes his plans only to discover that the rich are his OPPONENTS. To hold a banquet, he must install the poor as HELPERS. The comic (banquet) appears only in the rejection by the rich and invitation of the poor.

C. Going on a Journey (Matt. 25:14–30)

SUBJECT —————— OPPONENT

	SUBJECT	OPPONENT
expected	one-talent man	master
actual	master	one-talent man

We argued above that the parable's plot turns on the audience's evaluation of the master. The one-talent man preserves a stereotyped view of a hard and rapacious master, whereas his actions do not justify such a conclusion. If the audience believes the one-talent man, then the plot is tragic, with the servant as SUBJECT and the master as OPPONENT. Such an expected story is diagrammed above as "expected." But if the audience believes the master, then the story is a parable in which the master is SUBJECT and the one-talent man OPPONENT. The OBJECT, as the actual model makes clear, is the audience's esteem. But the audience can accept the "actual" investment only if it acknowledges that the master's stereotype (tragic) is incorrect and his treatment of the first two servants (comic) is his true mode of behavior.

D. A Father Had Two Sons (Luke 15:11–32)

The parable's plotting is complex and involves several distortions of the audience's expectation. It is divided into two sequences (younger and elder brothers), with a dominant plot of a father with two sons.

1) Younger Son's Sequence

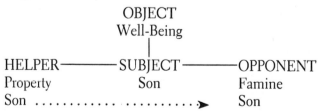

The father's division of property provides for his younger son's well-being, and installs the son as SUBJECT of the sequence.

His expected HELPER is the property and his own initiative, determination, and skill. But this is soon frustrated when the son becomes his own OPPONENT (along with famine, etc.). The only way to ensure his well-being is for the father to become his HELPER, which makes the father SUBJECT of the story rather than the younger son.

2) Elder Son's Sequence

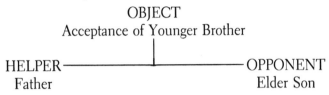

OBJECT
Acceptance of Younger Brother

HELPER————————————————OPPONENT
Father   Elder Son

The elder son's sequence follows the audience's expectation insofar as he is the expected OPPONENT. Only at the end where the father refuses to confirm the elder son as OPPONENT is the audience forced to reckon that it has been told a story other than the one it had expected. The expected story concerns the well-being of the younger son which can be diagrammed as follows:

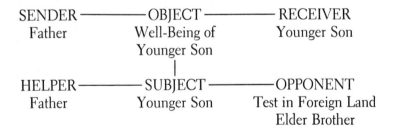

SENDER————————OBJECT————————RECEIVER
Father   Well-Being of   Younger Son
                Younger Son

HELPER—————————SUBJECT—————————OPPONENT
Father   Younger Son   Test in Foreign Land
                                     Elder Brother

But instead of this traditional story, the audience is told a story diagrammed as follows:

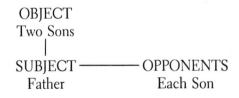

OBJECT
Two Sons

SUBJECT————————OPPONENTS
Father   Each Son

The audience not only must recognize that the parable is a different story than they had first thought, but also that the favorite younger son is an OPPONENT of the father. The elder son's opposition is ultimately directed not against the younger son but against the father as SUBJECT. To discover the parabolic comedy of two sons, the audience must abandon an expected plot and experience with the father tragic rejection by each son to appreciate joy at retaining both.

The actantial model has enabled us to represent in an abstract scheme the structure of four narrative parables. This process has shown that the plots are constrained or determined by a fundamental vision of Kingdom represented by our first thesis: the comic appears under the guise of tragedy. This vision (or world view) of Kingdom produces a consistent effect in the narrative structure: a reevaluation of an expected investment of the actantial model. The actantial motion is consistently from tragedy to comedy.

ONE-LINERS

Narrative parables as performances (sentences) were diagrammed with the help of the actantial model to disclose their underlying grammar. Our goal for one-liners is the same; they, too, are performances (sentences) with an underlying grammar. But the actantial model will not expose the grammar because there is no narrative. Therefore, we must look for another model.

In chapter 3 we saw that one-liners were related closely to proverbs and could be classified as parabolic proverbs. We followed William Beardslee's suggestions that the proverb as a form depends upon a stable cosmos, a world of predictability, which is subverted by Jesus' proverbs. Further, each proverb implies a traditional story which the proverb summarizes as insight. This was found to hold true of one-liners.

The implied story of proverbs suggests a correspondence to Lévi-Strauss's understanding of myth. The function of myth "is to provide a logical model capable of overcoming a contradiction."[19] An apparently irresoluble opposition between two terms is overcome by a third term capable of mediating both terms of opposition. Proverbs perform a similar function. In the proverb "spare the rod and spoil the child," the assumed common story is that of the spoiled, undisciplined child who grows up to be an unproductive adult. While from this communal, cultural experience is derived a proverbial insight, at the same time the proverb serves to mediate between opposing visions of parental love. Frequently a child is undisciplined because parents out of love do not wish to inflict pain. But the proverb sanctions a higher love by mediating the parental pain in the discipine of true love.

Insofar as one-liners partake of proverb they should be expected to exhibit a mediating function. To expose the mediating function in an abstract scheme, I propose an adaptation of Lévi-Strauss's mythical model for an analysis of one-liners.

SIGNIFIED   SIGNIFIER

(A)   (A_1)

C

B B_1

In this abstract scheme parentheses ( ) mean the term is unexpressed,[20] although frequently it can be deduced from or is implied by other expressed terms.[21] A and B represent primary, unresolved opposition. For one-liners primary opposition is between B, Kingdom of God as expressed in Jesus' symbol and (A) Kingdom of God in the audience's presupposition. A_1 and B_1 are images or metaphors associated with A and B respectively. C is an element of mediation which partakes of both A_1 and B_1. In the expected or implied story, C is an element of A_1 but in parable it receives a metaphorical reinvestment by being brought into association with B_1. This will emerge as the chief transformational rule of one-liners.[22]

The model is further divided into spheres of Signified and Signifier, as a way of indicating the relation of AB to A_1B_1. In Saussure's terminology the signified is a concept and signifier a sound-image, which are united into a sign.[23] The association in the sign effects the meaning. Saussure represents the unity with the following diagram:

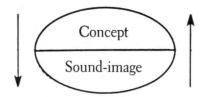

When applied to one-liners, the distinction accentuates both the unity of parable and symbol and their *mutual* interrelatedness. The referential motion is not simply from parable to symbol but is in both directions. This mutuality demands the unexpressed terms of the model in order to effect meaning.[24]

A.   Mustard Plant

SIGNIFIED	SIGNIFIER
(A Kingdom of God)	(A₁ Great Tree)

$$\text{C Shade}$$

B Kingdom of God	B₁ Mustard Plant

The parable, as do all four one-liners, announces as its Signified "Kingdom of God," which is represented as B. The topic is both known and unknown to the audience. It has certain traditional connotations within Israel's image stock whereby it is associated with other images and myths in her tradition. Those potential meanings remain unexpressed as (A). The speaker, by resorting to metaphor, seeks to reinvest the audience's understanding of Kingdom by bringing it into conjunction with his own. To put it simply, by parable he seeks to convert the audience both to his world view and to Kingdom.[25] (In constructing models for the other one-line parables we will not discuss the investment of the Signified AB, since the investment is identical to the one analyzed here.)

The investment of the Signifier will make evident the fundamental opposition at the level of Signified. In our discussion of the Mustard Plant the reference to "birds nesting in shade" was seen as an oblique reference to the Great Tree tradition. This verse is represented in our model as C Shade. Great Tree is invested A_1. As a Signifier of Kingdom Great Tree conjures up images which are contraries of Mustard Plant. The allusion to the Great Tree allows the Shade to mediate between Tree and Mustard Plant because it partakes of both images. Diachronically, the last line of the parable (Shade) belongs to the Great Tree tradition, but synchronically, within the parable, it has undergone a transformation: no longer is it the shade of the Great Tree but now the shade of a Mustard Plant. Thus shade mediates, not resolves, the opposition between A and B, two opposing views of Kingdom.

Just as the grammar of narrative parables was constrained by the thesis of the comic and tragic, so is the grammar of one-liners. From the viewpoint of the audience's Signified (A), the Mustard Plant B_1 is tragic, while the mediating agent Shade C is comic. This pattern recurs in all one-liners, reproducing in these parables the comic appearing in the guise of tragedy.

B.   Leaven

Signified	Signifier
(A Kingdom of God)	(A_1 Unleavened)
	C Three Measures
B Kingdom of God	B_1 Leaven

Leaven, with its connotations of moral corruption, is for the audience an inappropriate image. This opposition again signifies the deeper opposition at the level of Signified. The investment of B_1 as Leaven suggests that the unexpressed A_1 should be Unleavened. Given the association of Unleavened with the holy,[26] Leaven clearly implies its binary Unleavened.

The opposition between Leaven and its unexpressed contrary A_1, Unleavened, represents an unmediated opposition at the level of Signified. Mediation occurs in metaphor with the incorporation of three measures into the parable. Three measures in Israel is an image for a divine epiphany, a comic sign of the holy. But because as an image for the holy it can be incorporated into a parable about Leaven, it mediates between the two.

As in the construction of the Mustard Plant, the comic sign three measures is incorporated into the tragic sign, the Leaven. At the level of symbolic evaluation there is conflict, which the parabolic structure resolves. The conflict actually teases the mind to return to Dodd's definition of parable.

C. Fig Tree

SIGNIFIED	SIGNIFIER
(A Kingdom of God)	(A$_1$ Apocalyptic Blessing)
	C Fig Tree
B Kingdom of God	B$_1$ Summer

In our discussion we saw that this prominent tree of Palestine was associated with Yahweh's blessing for Israel. This made the parable's ending, with its naturalistic note of the coming of summer, quite jarring. Since the parable learned from the Fig Tree is the approach of summer, B$_1$ is invested as Summer and A$_1$ is invested with the image normally associated with Fig Tree, Apocalyptic Blessing. The parable poses an opposition between visions of Kingdom as Apocalyptic Blessing and as Summer. Fig Tree mediates the opposition. Associations with Fig Tree are transferred in parable to the approach of Summer, creating a tension at the level of symbolic evaluation.

For the audience, Summer is a tragic limitation of the coming Fig Tree since it denies its apocalyptic potential. Again we find the same pattern of transformation.

D. Seed Cast upon the Ground

SIGNIFIED	SIGNIFIER
(A Kingdom of God)	(A$_1$ Holy War)
	C Harvest
B Kingdom of God	B$_1$ Sabbatical

The organization of images here is identical to the Mustard Plant. The last line of both parables contains an allusion to an

Old Testament text whose context in parable contrasts strikingly to its Old Testament context. Just as the reference to "birds nesting in shade" mediates between Mustard Plant and Great Tree, so also the Joel quote operates in this parable. The quote is represented in the model as C Harvest. B_1, which is invested as Sabbatical, represents both *automatos* ("grows by itself") as well as the obvious passivity of the farmer. A_1 is invested as Holy War because of the mediating agent's context in Joel.

Harvest is the comic prospect but its synchronic shift demands a considerable risk on the audience's part. Diachronically the Joel context casts the harvest as an image for Holy War, but within the parable it is recast as a Harvest of passivity. The parable constructs a thickness of passive images—the farmer's passivity and the land on Sabbatical. These two images on the surface appear to be in contradiction, but combined with the Joel quotation they create a striking dissimilarity to the notion of the Holy War. For the audience to enjoy the Harvest it must surrender its pretext of joining Yahweh's mighty army and leave itself tragically vulnerable to the forces of evil.

A DEEP GRAMMAR

In pursuing the analogy of sentence/implied grammar, we have treated two types of parables as two different types of sentences. We have diagrammed narrative and one-line parables. From the diagrams a consistent transformational rule for each type emerged. The narrative parable rule is: An actant is transformed by being shifted within the actantial model from an expected to an unexpected position. Usually the motion is along the axis of power. For example, the Samaritan is not the expected OPPONENT, but the unexpected HELPER. For one-liners there is also a transformational rule: A comic mediating agent is transformed by incorporation into a synchronic context that opposes its former diachronic context.[27] For example, the Shade of the Mustard Plant is no longer the Shade of the Great Tree.

These consistent transformations are demanded by Thesis I concerning the comic appearing under the guise of tragedy. It represents Jesus' vision of World as expressed in Kingdom. This suggests that the grammar for the two types of parables is supported or constrained by a deeper, unifying grammar. To return to the analogy of language, the grammar of an individual sentence does not fully explain a sentence's meaning effect, much less the meaning of a series of sentences. Grammar is a vehicle for expressing other structures of meaning. A poet is constrained by the grammar of poetry (e.g., rhymes, form, etc.), but he is even further constrained by his poetic vision, which is a sort of deeper grammar. In the parables the grammar of narrative and one-liners is organized in a particular way because of Jesus' vision of Kingdom. Can this vision, expressed propositionally in Thesis I, be formalized in an abstract model that will account for the constraints upon narrative and one-line grammar?

In diagramming one-liners a consistent pattern appeared. Between A (the audience's view of Kingdom) and B_1 (parable as Signifier of Jesus' view of Kingdom) there was always a relation of opposition. For example, in the audience's vision of Kingdom the appropriate Signifier was Great Tree, whereas the parable used a Mustard Plant. This can be diagrammed as follows:

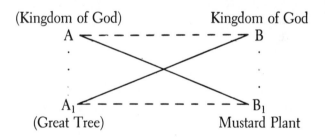

From our previous analysis of the parable we can deduce the following relations in this model:

1) A and B are contraries
2) A_1 and B_1 are contraries

(Relation of contraries is indicated by – – – –.) A contrary states that A is *not* B. It would be overstating the evidence to argue that the audience's vision of Kingdom is the opposite of Jesus', rather it simply is *not* the Kingdom. Because A is not B, it is impossible to directly mediate Jesus' vision of Kingdom and that of his audience. Tree and Mustard Plant as images are also not opposites but contraries—they are *not* each other.

3) A and B_1 are opposites
4) B and A_1 are opposites

(Relation of opposites will be indicated by————.) Opposites negate each other, e.g., $+1$ negates -1. The relation of opposition is between Signified and opposing Signifier. For example, Mustard Plant as metaphor for Kingdom is opposite of the audience's expectation. By burlesquing and poking fun at the audience's Kingdom, it denies (negates) the reality of that Kingdom.

5) A implies A_1
6) B implies B_1

(Relation of implication will be indicated by . . . .) A relation of implication is that A implies the existence of A_1, e.g., husband implies wife. This relation is deduced from the relation between Signified and Signifier. If there were no relation of implication between the symbol Kingdom and the Mustard Plant then it could not be a Signifier for that symbol.

This model of interrelations can be worked out for the one-liners by shifting vertically the mediating model used above. No further explanation of investment is needed as it is self-explanatory from the formation of the model for the Mustard Plant.[28]

Leaven

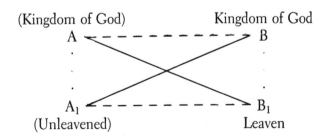

Fig Tree

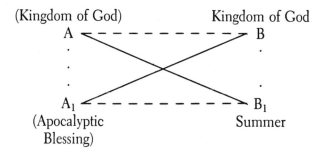

Seed Cast upon the Ground

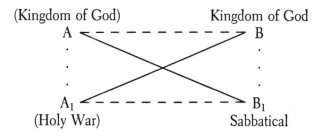

If one-liners can be organized into a coherent pattern of relations, does the structure of narrative parables reflect the same
pattern? In narrative parables we observed a consistent difference
between the audience's expected investment of the actantial
model and its actual investment. The difference between expected and actual investment is similar to the contraries in one-
liners between Jesus' Signifier and the expected Signifier (e.g.,
expected Great Tree/actual Mustard Plant). With this as a clue
we can invest our model with the actants from Jerusalem to
Jericho. The audience expected the Samaritan to be the actant
OPPONENT, but instead in the actual narrative he became the
actant HELPER. If we invest this reversal of expectation as the
contraries A_1 – – – – – B_1 we would arrive at the following
model:

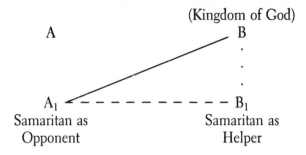

In the model B is in parentheses because this parable (and all
narrative parables) does not have Kingdom as an expressed Signified. Nevertheless, B represents Jesus' symbol. A remains un-
invested, although parallel with one-liners, A is the audience's
vision of Kingdom. The three terms invested do account for the
organization of the actantial model of the parable. Jesus' vision
of Kingdom does imply Samaritan as HELPER, while its contrary Samaritan as OPPONENT is the opposite of Jesus' vision
of Kingdom. (Thus A is Kingdom from the audience's viewpoint; i.e, this view implies Samaritan as OPPONENT.) Comparing this investment of the model with that of the one-liners
confirms the analysis and indicates that the models are isomorphic, i.e., have the same form.

A similar investment of the model can be worked out for our
other three narrative parables using the transformation in the
actantial model to indicate the contraries.

A Great Banquet

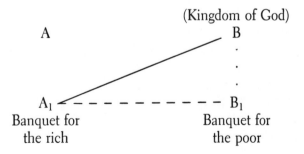

Going on a Journey

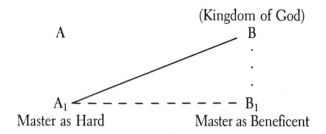

A   (Kingdom of God)
                 B

A_1 B_1
Master as Hard   Master as Beneficent

A Father Had Two Sons

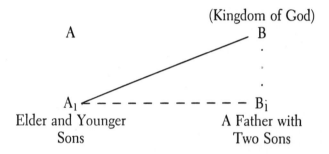

A   (Kingdom of God)
                 B

A_1 B_1
Elder and Younger   A Father with
Sons   Two Sons

The ability to use a single model to describe all eight parables so that all terms and relations are isomorphic suggests the probability of a single investment that can account for and unite the eight individual investments. Such an investment will have to be sufficiently general and abstract to account for the particular investments in previous models.

The investment of A and B is obvious.

Jesus' Symbol   Audience's Symbol
Kingdom of God   Kingdom of God
B – – – – – – – – – – – – –A

The investment of B poses no real problem since that investment has remained constant throughout eight parables: Jesus' symbol, Kingdom of God. The contrary A has been invested in the previous models as the audience's vision of Kingdom. From the viewpiont of B, A is non-Kingdom and, while general and abstract, such a definition or investment is not very helpful. Their vision of Kingdom, as evidenced in the previous chapters, is frozen, static, and sedimented. I propose to summarize this vision with the term "The Accepted." This contrasts with Jesus' use of Kingdom as fluid and plastic, as a true tensive symbol. This leads to a reinvestment of the contraries AB.

$$\text{Kingdom of God} \qquad\qquad \text{The Accepted}$$
$$B\text{-- -- -- -- -- -- -- -- -- -- --}A$$

An investment of B_1 -- -- -- -- -- A_1 is determined by previous investments of those terms in the parables and the ability to fulfill the definition of the term. The following chart indicates the investment of B_1 -- -- -- -- -- A_1 in previous models.

B_1	A_1
Samaritan as Helper	Samaritan as Opponent
Banquet for Poor	Banquet for Rich
Master as Beneficent	Master as Hard
Father with Two Sons	Elder and Younger Sons
Mustard Plant	Great Tree
Leaven	Unleavened
Summer	Apocalyptic Blessing
Sabbatical	Holy War

In seeking sufficiently abstract and general terms to represent the investments of A_1 and B_1, I propose to invest B_1 as "Reality" and A_1 as "Illusion." From the viewpoint of B (Jesus' symbol Kingdom) the individual investments of B_1 indicate what is real, the true metaphors of Kingdom, what makes the Kingdom real, whereas the contrary signifiers are illusionary and lead to the non-Kingdom, The Accepted. The complete model is as follows:

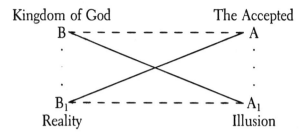

In investing the model the determining term is B, Jesus' symbol, Kingdom of God. Not only does it determine the perspective for other terms, but it receives specificity and effects meaning by its relation to other terms in the model. Furthermore, the audience's organization of the model is the exact opposite of Jesus'. From the viewpoint of A (the audience's expectation of Kingdom) Jesus' Signifiers are Illusion.

What is the gain in this theoretic construction, and how does it advance an understanding of Kingdom? First, the model provides us with a way of *representing* the accumulated insights of parables without reduction to discursive propositions. Second, the dynamic interrelation between the model's terms and the representational modality indicates how meaning is effected in the specific performance of each parable. Just as the grammar of a sentence is not the meaning of a sentence but only an indication of how it works (or effects meaning), so our model indicates *only* how parables effect meaning.

We have followed a deductive method in arriving at the model and its investment. Such a method's value is that the categories are derived from the parables, not from outside. Now we will utilize our model inductively to gain greater specificity concerning the contraries Reality–Illusion. We will do this by reviewing the five theses developed in chapters 2 and 3.

A. The comic appears under the guise of tragedy

In the present chapter we already have seen that this thesis represents a primary constraint upon the actantial model of narrative parables and the transformation of the mediating agent in one-liners. In chapters 2 and 3 the thesis characterized the audience when asked to abandon its known World, risk its loss, to achieve the World of parable. While Kingdom is itself a comic term, its tragic dimension is illustrated graphically by the above model: when Reality is defined as the opposite of The Accepted, the audience is in a tragic situation since from the perspective of parable it finds itself in an unreal world. The reversal theme, so frequently associated with parables, is part of this dynamic. For Kingdom to function as a truly tensive, comic symbol, it must have a destructive, tragic element within it, to destroy the assured and to point out the real. The dynamic between comedy and tragedy within the parables can be represented as follows:

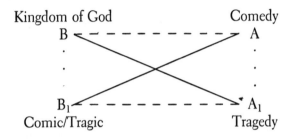

Paradoxically, although Kingdom is a comic symbol, Comedy is the contrary of Kingdom, just as Tragedy is its opposite. Kingdom implies a comic/tragic perception as parables argue.

B.   Grace comes to those who have no other alternative

This thesis was exemplified by the plight of the man in the ditch in Jerusalem to Jericho. He must accept the Samaritan's ministry. Similarly, in Going on a Journey the one-talent man is blinded by his stereotyped impression of the master; he does not see that his only alternative is a benevolent master. In A Father Had Two Sons, the audience's acceptance of grace depends upon their acceptance of the elder son, of seeing that his role has granted him and them no other alternative. For the audience to accept the images mustard seed and leaven as appropriate metaphors for Kingdom is to enter the ditch metaphorically. Finally, in Seed Cast upon the Ground, the grace of *kairos* is realization that Kingdom is the time when no time is left.

This review suggests that within the terms of our model, a further investment is possible. Grace as implied by Kingdom can be represented as B_1 and its contrary (A_1) would be status, the maintenance of what already is.

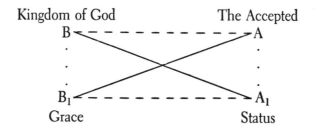

To receive the Kingdom's grace demands an abandonment of one's perceived place or status in reality. Kingdom is an inversion of the value scale by which one normally navigates through what is perceived to be the everyday World. In the World of Kingdom hard masters are not hard, Jews become dependent upon Samaritans, and the Kingdom works its way like leaven, corrupting all it touches.

C.   In the world of the parable the religious and the secular are congruent

This thesis primarily indicated the rejection of allegory in favor of parable. Jesus' images are natural, secular images. They are not steno-referents to some outside reality. The key to their openness is within them.[29] In the Mustard Plant the allegory of the Great Tree is rejected and in the Fig Tree the image association with Yahweh's blessing is demythologized. But the parable's obvious rejection of allegory should not lead us to be blinded to the images' polyvalency. Leaven, even as a secular image, has overtones of moral corruption. The image's diachronic heritage is part of its synchronic association. A Father Had Two Sons definitely has two meaning levels as story. It belongs to the general, transcultural stories of sibling rivalry, and furthermore, since this motif has been applied to Israel, the parable is also pertinent to Israel's self-understanding.

What underlying organization of the images of the parable

demands this congruity of the religious and secular? Ultimately
Jesus' vision of Kingdom predicates an experience of wholeness
or, negatively, non-duality. Kingdom as Yahweh's claim is abso-
lute and does not allow for divisions. Reality is claimed and
thereby whole. The contrary to this is Reality as Divided, which
is implied in the term The Accepted. Or to put it in the image of
our original investment, division is illusion.

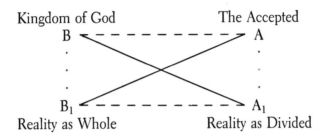

The Accepted of necessity divides Reality; it proclaims who is
in, who is out; who is saved, who is not; the sons of light, the
sons of darkness, etc. The parables' consistent rejection of accepted values results from their fundamental vision of wholeness—the reversal leads to a vision of the inappropriateness of
Them/Us.

This also explains two other factors in the parables: the rejection of apocalyptic images and the non-specificity of the Kingdom's temporality.[30] Apocalyptic both divides and predicts, and
clearly belongs within the terms A . . . A_1, The Accepted . . .
Reality as Divided. Predictability violates fundamental symbols
within parables. The Kingdom is *kairos*, not *chronos*; it does not
divide, it heals: a father had two sons; it is summer.

D.   The World of the hearer is questioned by the World of the parable

Running throughout the discussion of parables, this thesis describes how a parable operates as heuristic device. The rejection
of stereotypes (e.g., the hard and cruel master) or the use of
inappropriate images (leaven) is part of the parable's World-
questioning.

Such World-questioning leads, as observed above, to two ultimate models in opposition, Jesus' and the audience's investment. For the audience, what Jesus sees as reality is illusion. No wonder the parable questions the hearer's World; its symbolic organization is the opposite of the expected organization.

E.   Faith is the ability to trust the depiction of World in the parable

Three elements contribute to this thesis: faith in the World of parable, faith in the parable teller, and the parable teller's faith in his own vision.

Two parables sketched faith's dimensions in the parabolic World. In Going on a Journey, the one-talent man fails his test when asked to make his judgment on the master's actions rather than his stereotype. Faith would demand that he trust the master to be fair even before evidence of what the master will do. In Leaven, other dimensions of faith are evident. The audience is asked to have faith both in the metaphor and in the teller. How do they know that he has intuited the correct metaphor for Kingdom? By what audacity does the teller use leaven to describe God's activity?

This leads to a final investment of our model: the contrary of faith is ideology.

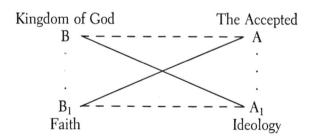

$$\begin{array}{ll} \text{Kingdom of God} & \text{The Accepted} \\ \quad \text{B} & \quad \text{A} \\ \quad \text{B}_1 & \quad \text{A}_1 \\ \quad \text{Faith} & \quad \text{Ideology} \end{array}$$

An investment of knowledge as a contrary of faith is inappropriate because this is not exactly the problematic of faith and knowledge. Ideology suggests the predictable and knowable, not on the basis of evidence (which would be faith in terms of the parable), but on the basis of what is predetermined. For this reason parables reject an apocalyptic world view. Because faith is a contrary of ideology, Jesus stands at odds with aspects of his culture which would have identified the two.

A GENERATIVE MODEL

As a final step in our formalization of a parabolic grammar, the models used to analyze our theses can be organized into a unified model that represents the interrelatedness of the various models.

Kingdom of God

Reality   – – – – – – – –   Illusion

Comedy through   Comedy or
Tragedy   – – – – – – – –   Tragedy

Grace   – – – – – – –   Status

Reality as   Reality as
Whole   – – – – – – – –   Divided

Faith   – – – – – – – –   Ideology

The Accepted

Kingdom of God and The Accepted have been placed at either end of the model to indicate that these two form a semantic axis which generates the arrangement of images in the parables.[31] That is, the interaction of these two terms generates the most basic constraints represented by the series of contraries. The interactions of contraries effect meaning in the performance of particular parables. The model generates the parables in the same sense as the rules of grammar generate a sentence.

A review of our method will highlight the model's generative and dynamic function.

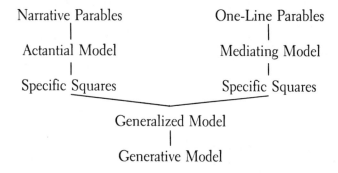

We began with a study of eight parables which represent a corpus (though incomplete) of Jesus' parables. For each narrative parable an actantial model was developed and together they exhibited a consistent pattern. Lévi-Strauss's mythical model was adapted for the one-liners, and again a consistent pattern emerged. The oppositions uncovered by these two models were organized in turn by a single model, the so-called square of opposition. This produced an abstract and general model whose terms and interactions could explain the organization of more specific models. Finally, this generalized pattern was reinterpreted in light of the five theses developed in the study of individual parables.

The ultimate symbol in the parables remains the Kingdom of God. Everything in our analysis confirms this. *But we also have discovered that Kingdom is a symbol of such deep significance that it remains beyond definition or immediate expression.* It is both so deep and so generalized that it can stand for the entire parabolic World. It generates and constrains other images in its effort to break through and create meaning.

These models should not be thought of as having an ontological status. They are models indicating the potential for dynamic interaction of the images within parables. They try to explain why parables take the form they do. They serve to help organize and generate a wholistic, integrated insight into the parabolic corpus. If the reader can say, "I don't understand, but I see," then the models have served their purpose.

The study of selected parables has concluded that parables do imply a unified system that can with some precision be specified. We now turn our attention to other elements of the Jesus tradition to see if those elements cohere with the model of parables.

NOTES

1. The ultimate referent of a parable is always once removed insofar as Kingdom of God as a symbol has itself a referent. Susan Wittig, "A Theory of Multiple Meanings," *Semeia* 9 (1977):75–103, provides a cogent discussion of this aspect of parabolic sign.

2. On the use of the term "manifestation," see Daniel Patte, *What Is Structural Exegesis?* Guides to Biblical Scholarship (Philadelphia: Fortress Press, 1976), p. 23.

3. *Method in Theology* (New York: Herder and Herder, 1972), p. 64. One of Lonergan's major contributions to epistemology has been his *Insight* (New York: Basic Books, 1957).

4. Lonergan, *Insight*, p. 185.

5. Richard A. Edwards, *The Sign of Jonah in the Theology of the Evangelists and Q*, Studies in Biblical Theology 18, 2d series (London: SCM Press, 1971), has studied the various pericopes of Jesus' rejection of signs and concluded that Mark 8:11–12 has the highest claim for authenticity.

6. *Insight*, p. 9.

7. Ibid., p. 5

8. Ibid.

9. Ibid.

10. As this chapter tries to articulate this "hint," the reader is warned not to be fooled into believing that one is being presented with any more than a mere hint. Franz Kafka's warning must be borne in mind: "All these parables really set out to say merely that the incomprehensible is incomprehensible, and we know that already. But the cares we have to struggle with everyday: that is a different matter" (*Parables and Paradoxes* [New York: Schocken Books, 1961], p. 11).

11. The word "suggestive" is chosen deliberately, since it is impossible to prove in advance that a particular model will be appropriate for analyzing parables. One of the important results of Gödel's proof is that a phenomenon is not understandable within its own terms but must be explained by a higher set of terms. This should warn us against any attempt at reduction of parables. To understand parables one must increase their complexity by incorporating them within a more complex structuring system. For the significance of Gödel's proof cf., Jean Piaget, *Structuralism*, trans. Chaninah Maschler (New York: Harper Torch Books, 1970), pp. 32ff.

12. *Course in General Linguistics*, trans. Wade Baskin (New York: Philosophical Library, 1959), pp. 7–17; Edgar McKnight, *Meaning in Texts* (Philadelphia: Fortress Press, 1978), pp. 97–98; Robert Scholes, *Structuralism in Literature* (New Haven: Yale University Press, 1974), p. 14.

13. This corresponds to parable as insight. As the actualization of Jesus' insight, a particular parable is *parole*, but it is *langue* for the hearer, i.e., a potential for meaning that awaits actualization by the hearer's performance.

14. For a convenient discussion see Patte, *What Is Structural Exegesis?* pp. 42f. The use of these models is related analogically to diagrams in sentence grammar. It is a way of visualizing the construction of a sentence. But there is one very important difference: there is little argument over whether a verb is a verb, while the identification of actants is very controversial. (Patte does not seem to appreciate the controversial and interpretative aspect in the identification of actants, sequences, etc.) This demands a recognition of the importance and necessity of the reader's competence. In defense of our method, we are not attempting to explain the construction of a parable by means of an actantial model (inductive method) but are using the model to clarify previous readings (deductive method).

15. Ibid., p. 42.

16. John Dominic Crossan, *The Dark Interval* (Niles, Ill.: Argus Communications, 1975), p. 66, argues that the conflict between what he calls the structure of expectation and the structure of expression "is the heart of the parabolic event," part of its deep structure. Crossan has clearly seen the importance of reconstructing the audience's expectation in order to understand a parable's meaning effect. But he has mistaken a technique for a fundamental opposition. The conflict of expectation with actual expression is a technique for exposing the

deeper opposition between visions of reality. This will become evident in our analysis.

17. Investment means the actualization of an actant or function.

18. Cf. above, chap. 3, p. 70. It should be noted that priest and Levite move from potential Helpers to Opponents.

19. "The Structural Study of Myth," in *Structural Anthropology*, trans. Claire Jacobson and Brooke Schoepf (New York: Basic Books, 1963), p. 226.

20. Throughout the remainder of the chapter parentheses (   ) in models indicate unexpressed in actual performance.

21. One of the functions of a model is its ability to predict. This is so because a model represents in abstract form the potential of actualization.

22. It is important to distinguish the mediating element from Jülicher's *tertium comparationis*. For Jülicher and subsequent interpreters in the simile A is like B, the interpreter sought the element of comparison or commonality between A and B. This became the point of the parable. We have rejected such an understanding of parable. Our mediating term is synchronically transformed in the parable itself.

23. *General Linguistics*, p. 66. Saussure refers to the relation between Signified and Signifier as "psychological"; within the context of our discussion I would prefer to accentuate the relation as imaginative. See Robert C. Tannehill, *The Sword of His Mouth*, Semeia Studies (Missoula, Mont: Scholars Press and Philadelphia: Fortress Press, 1975), 21–27.

24. It should be remembered that Kingdom of God as a symbol is itself a Signifier with an unexpressed Signified. This is part of the density of signification referred to at the beginning of this chapter.

25. These parables are not simply polemical, but because they are metaphorical they imply a newness of vision in what is to be communicated. Jeremias's contention concerning the polemical character of parables results from a misapprehension of their metaphorical character.

26. Ernst Lohmeyer, *Evangelium des Matthäus* (Göttingen: Vandenhoeck & Ruprecht, 1958), p. 220, sees the parable of the leaven as an attack upon the temple and its cult.

27. In this formulation diachronic indicates the expected context while synchronic, the unexpected.

28. The model, at which we have arrived deductively, is the so-called square of opposition. For A. J. Greimas this represents a logical picturing of an elementary structure of signification, i.e., from a log-

ical point of view it represents the most elementary relations possible. A. J. Greimas and F. Rastier, "The Interaction of Semiotic Constraints," *Yale French Studies* 41 (1969): 86–105. See the helpful comments of Edgar McKnight, *Meaning in Texts*, pp. 170ff. For some important comments on the limitations of Greimas's program, see Jonathan Culler, *Structuralist Poetics* (Ithaca: Cornell University Press, 1975), chap. 4.

29. Even when some parables, e.g., Mustard Plant, Seed Cast upon the Ground, refer to Old Testament texts, synchronically the quoted text is transformed.

30. This theme will be dealt with in greater detail in the next chapter.

31. In identifying this model as "generative" I risk confusion with the program of Erhardt Güttgemanns. To the reader familiar with Güttgemanns, it should be obvious that my enterprise, although related, is quite distinct. I would mark three important points of difference. First, I have followed a deductive method, proceeding from readings of the text (chaps. 2 and 3) to the attempt to diagram the texts based upon clues found in the text itself. Secondly, since we have followed a deductive method we stress the subjective, interpretative role in the investment of models. Finally, the model and investment is not capable of being used as a criterion to stand in judgment upon the preaching of the church. If one believes that knowledge of the grammar of a performance allows the creation of other performances, that one is very naive. A representative collection of Güttgemanns's essays in English can be found in *Semeia* 6 (1976), trans. William G. Doty and Norman R. Petersen; *Candid Questions Concerning Gospel Form Criticism*, trans. William Doty, Pittsburgh Theological Monograph Series 26 (Pittsburgh: Pickwick Press, 1979). Again I would refer the reader to the brief remarks of Edgar McKnight, *Meaning in Texts*, pp. 269–70, whose conclusion I would support.

5

PARABLES, SAYINGS, AND DEEDS

At the deepest level Jesus' parables exhibit a consistent pattern of arrangement, which we have represented in a generative model. We also observed, by means of William Beardslee's analysis, similarities between proverbs and one-liners. In this chapter, that relation will be pursued into an examination of the possible relation of Jesus' sayings and deeds to the parables. Is the structural model underlying the parables present in this material?

In selecting the material to be examined, the interpreter must determine what in the synoptic Gospels to study and how to organize it. Our procedure will be to take soundings rather than to mount an exhaustive study. Norman Perrin has listed a group of sayings which he argued most scholars would accept as the minimum that could be isolated as authentic Jesus material.[1] We will accept his list. These sayings have been authenticated by means of the negative criterion, i.e., a saying is authentic if it comes from neither the church nor Judaism. According to Perrin this expresses Jesus' distinctiveness,[2] but as Leander Keck has warned, an exclusive use of the negative criterion can lead to a picture of Jesus that accents the dissimilar, non-Jewish elements. The texture and complexity of Jesus as first-century Jew may be missed.[3] In a study as limited as ours, Keck's warning has particular relevance. Also, Perrin's list deals exclusively with the sayings tradition, omitting the actions or deeds of the historical Jesus, e.g., his association with the outcast.[4] Paul Achtemeier has scored the New Hermeneutic for its failure to pay attention to Jesus' exorcisms and healings.[5] Both of these warnings demand that we expand our study to include a consideration of Jesus' actions.[6]

After selecting material to examine, a critic must organize it into intelligible units. Frequently the organization is dictated by an outside system. Hans Conzelmann's encyclopedia article, *Jesus*, uses systematic categories to organize the section on Jesus' teaching.[7]

The content of Jesus' teaching

a) Fundamentals (Law, Scripture Tradition, Israel)
b) Concept of God
c) The Will of God (Ethics)
d) The Announcement of the Kingdom of God

There is nothing intrinsically wrong with such a method. The development of categories to fashion a discussion is a normal and necessary process, unless the interpreter is a parrot. The question concerns their appropriateness for the topic. The categories must always be adapted to suit the phenomenon. We have organized the material along formal lines and allowed the material to suggest its own categories. Thus the only grouping for parables was form: narrative parables and one-liners.

The same procedure will guide this chapter. We will discuss in turn Proverbs, Parenetical Proverbs, Beatitudes, Kingdom Sayings, Lord's Prayer, and Actions. Like parables, the first three groups are *meshalim*. The Kingdom Sayings form a coherent group because of the use of Kingdom of God in the sayings. Because of its variety of themes, the Lord's Prayer is an important piece of evidence. The final grouping will be a set of actions thought to be typical of Jesus.

We will focus on the correlation of the six groups with the structures underlying the parables. The correlation will be tested by the use of the generative model developed in the previous chapter. It represents a generalized, abstract model for organizing the parable's images. The model is as follows:

Kingdom of God

A		B	
Reality	$-------$	Illusion	1
Comedy through Tragedy	$-----$	The Comic or The Tragic	2
Grace	$-------$	Status	3
Reality as Whole	$-------$	Reality as Divided	4
Faith	$-------$	Ideology	5

The Accepted

Kingdom of God and The Accepted form the semantic axis of the model. Its terms derive their meaning both from their inter-relations (i.e., the terms are mutually defining) and from the specific images which they represent. The analysis of those images and the investment of the model were developed in the previous chapter. The interrelation of the terms can be described as follows.

1) Terms in the same column are related by implication; they imply each other (these are the terms joined by a dotted line), e.g., Grace implies Reality as Whole, and vice versa.
2) Terms joined by $-----$ are contraries; e.g., Reality and Illusion are contraries.
3) Terms on different lines are opposites; e.g., Grace on Line 3 is the opposite of Reality as Divided on Line 4.

Specific investments of the model will be capitalized throughout this chapter. This has no special significance except to alert the reader that the word is representing a term from the model. Since we arrived at the model deductively from a study of the parables, we will now ask whether the model can accommodate the six categories of material.

PROVERBS

Following William Beardslee's work on proverbs, we have suggested that one-liners are proverbial parables since they share with proverbs intensification of insight. As Semitic literary forms, narrative parables, one-liners, and proverbs are all *meshalim*. Because of a close formal relationship with parables, proverbs should exhibit similar structural features.

A proverb, typical of folk or popular literature, is by its very nature pre-discursive. It forces upon the hearer a cluster of insights about an ordered track of repeatable human experience,[8] resulting from the distillation of a common story. The proverb "Spare the rod and spoil the child" presumes a common human experience. Its truth is its practicality as an insightful summary of a lesson drawn from the repeated experience. In this sense the proverb is pre-discursive, i.e., it is prior to the development of systematic thought. At some point it demands the development of systematic thought.[9]

Because of its pre-discursiveness, a proverb's chief semantic function is the compelling of insight. According to Beardslee, it is a more direct or immediate form than the parable, which tends to be indirect.[10] Thus a proverb's focus is more specific. Nevertheless, because of their similarities with parables, proverbs offer a promising beginning for expanding the application of our model to other forms of Jesus' language.

Proverb is not concerned with the individual qua individual but has a "practical reference to the concrete behavior of a man among his fellow men, i.e., it is direct."[11] In Jewish Wisdom this led to a moralization of proverbs,[12] or what might better be called a parenetical concern. Since proverb derives its concentrated insight from a repeated human experience, the insight requests a certain performance on behalf of the hearer. For "Spare the rod and spoil the child," the demanded performance is discipline. To address its parenetical dimensions, we have isolated this type of proverb as a separate group.

Beardslee argues that a distinctive mutation of proverb occurs in the synoptic tradition, a mutation he presumes derives from Jesus.[13] The typical synoptic proverb so intensifies Wisdom's insight that it attacks the project of making a continuous whole out of one's existence. It undermines the reliability of common sense, the very presupposition of the traditional proverb. For Beardslee, the synoptic proverb makes a way of life out of challenging the project of making a whole of one's existence.[14]

Paradox and hyperbole are the strategies for this intensification. Beardslee arranges a group of proverbs in a rough scale between antithesis and true paradox. A typical antithesis is "everyone who exalts himself will be humbled, and he who humbles himself with be exalted" (Luke 14:11). As an example of paradox he selects "Whoever loses his life will preserve it" (Luke 17:33).[15] The hyperbolical proverbs also are arranged on a scale of intensity. An example of lesser hyperbole is "The foxes have holes, and birds of the air have nests; but the Son of man has nowhere to lay his head" (Matt. 8:20). For intensive hyperboles he takes as an example "Love your enemies, do good to those who hate you" (Luke 6:27).[16]

Beardslee's scale indicates continuity and diversity within the proverbs themselves.[17] It is simply not true that all of Jesus' proverbs are intense and radical in the extreme. Beardslee, by means of his classification, identifies a corpus of proverbs and provides an impetus for their consideration as a group.[18]

Paradoxical Proverbs (Luke 14:11; Mark 10:31; Luke 17:33)

These three proverbs, of which the last one is genuine paradox, presume the story of the common-sense observation that the proud frequently fall. But in the last proverb the insight has been intensified to the point that it reaches paradox. Here the project to make a whole of one's life has fallen apart.

Hyperbolical Proverbs (Mark 10:25; Luke 9:60)

Hyperbole operates differently in each proverb. In the first, hyperbole is in the comparison—the passing of a camel through

the eye of a needle. But at the same time the hyperbolical comparison attacks the common-sense assumption that riches are a
blessing from God. In the second proverb, the absurdity of the
image is hyperbolic. How can the dead bury the dead?

Inappropriate Proverbs (Mark 3:24–26, 27)

A third group of proverbs in the synoptic tradition operate, I
believe, by means of an inappropriate image. We have seen in
the parables (e.g., Leaven) that Jesus was fond of using such
images. Mark 3:27 and 3:24–6 are good examples of this strategy. Both proverbs, which originally circulated separately,[19] presume a common observation: the strong man must be disarmed
or tricked to be defeated, and in unity there is strength. But
when brought into conjunction with the symbol Kingdom of
God they are inappropriate. Should one speak of Kingdom as
plundering a strong man? The inappropriateness is heightened
in the second proverb in its third comparison. Perrin suggests
that it deals with the myth of the eschatological war[20] but the
proverb insists that what one is witnessing in the collapse of
Satan is Satan fighting Satan! It is not a war of good versus
evil with good triumphing, but evil fighting evil. This proverb paradoxically compounds the inappropriateness of the
images.

As proverbs, the sayings verbalize pre-discursive insights into
the experience of Kingdom. What accounts for the exaggeration
and intensification? It is generated by the same model underlying the parables. In seeing the hearer's World as Illusion, and
that Illusion as the opposite of authentic experience of Kingdom, Jesus is forced to verbally attack the root of World, to
destroy the horizon of meaning that grants the hearer surety.
The proverb exposes one's life as a life of Illusion. Everyday
moorings must be loosened to apprehend Kingdom. "Leave the
dead to bury their own" attacks the very root of one's normal
responsibilities. The normal proverb demands a predictable
World, one in which the dead are buried by their kin; but in the
Kingdom the dead's kin are the dead.

The unmasking of Illusion is also to be seen in the paradox,
"Whoever seeks to gain his life will lose it, but whoever loses
his life will preserve it." As a proverb it forces one to let go

imaginatively of the thing held most dear, life itself. But so exposed, one faces radically the ruling activity of God. Within the generative model, preserving life is the ultimate Status. To get into the ditch is to lose one's life and thereby be exposed to Status's contrary, Grace. The paradox of losing one's life "makes sense" when it is seen that it is part of the same generative structure as that of the parables. To lose one's life is to lose one's Status and thus be exposed to Grace, to the Kingdom.[21] The generative model demonstrates that the saying is not an absurdist attack on the everyday world but, as part of a larger network of relations, has a positive aspect: the loss of Status is the gaining of Grace.

The proverb of a kingdom divided against itself illustrates another correlation of proverbs with the generative model. Assuming that the proverb's *Sitz im Leben* is the controversy over Jesus' exorcisms, Perrin and others argue that it expresses the myth of the eschatological war.[22] This immediate context is probably correct, but Mark's use of the saying has obscured its true intention. In the Marcan context Jesus is the strong man who binds Satan and brings his kingdom to an end.[23] But closer attention to the image suggests that it does not vindicate this usage. The first two parts of the proverb are common enough— in unity there is strength. But how then does the last part apply to the Kingdom's coming? Surely its coming implies the end of Satan's. Therefore the hearer is forced to ask, is Satan destroying himself, or is he united and not coming to an end? The third line of the proverb forces a hearer to look around and see Satan in disarray, but to see Satan in disarray one must first abandon an Ideology of Kingdom as good defeating Satan as evil. Once that Ideology is abandoned, its contrary Faith sees the mysterious ruling activity of God in Satan rising up against Satan.[24]

Parenetical Proverbs (Mark 7:15; Matthew 5:39–41; Luke 6:27–28)

Formally these three sayings are proverbs, but Perrin is right to classify them as parenetical.[25] They achieve their intensity by means of hyperbole, which dispels the Illusionary World in which the hearer dwells to make Reality apparent. They are parenetical because they impinge directly upon everyday life and belong with the moralizing proverbs of Jewish Wisdom.[26] But instead of providing insight on how to cope with one's daily existence, they threaten existence with chaos. To follow any one of these sayings as a guide to everyday life would destroy common sense.

And yet the sayings are literally true;[27] hyperbolic exaggeration occurs not simply for effect—the speaker is not setting up an extreme position only to eventually compromise with a common-sense understanding. Literally, he perceives the logic of this World to be wrong and attacks it. The hyperbole exposes a new logic, a new common sense. To abandon the Ideology of Wisdom's moralizing tendency is to have Faith in a new order of Reality, which is granted in a radical experience of God's ruling activity.

Mark 7:15 attacks Judaism's ritual cleanliness[28] by radically placing the responsibility for defilement not outside but inside man. Perrin has argued that this saying "completely denies a fundamental presupposition of Jewish religion: the distinction between the sacred and the secular."[29] Perrin is both right and wrong. While one should question whether such a division is a fundamental assumption of Jewish religion,[30] what the proverb does attack is the common-sense observation of Reality as Divided—into heaven and earth, sacred and profane, etc. The insight that generates this saying follows from an experience of Kingdom as a healing reality (Reality as Whole). It is man who divides reality, makes the things outside him unclean. For God all is clean.

The other two parenetical sayings (Matt. 5:39–41; Luke 6:27–28[31]), as attacks upon the common-sense World, expose the hearer to tragedy through hyperbole. These two sayings are related to the Comic–Tragic structure of parables. They force the hearer to perceive the risk of Tragedy, of being slapped again and again, of losing all one's clothes, of loving an enemy—to perceive these as the way to the Comedy of the Kingdom.[32]

This brief analysis of a group of proverbs has allowed us to see that these *meshalim* can be understood in terms of the same generative model that underlies the parables. The model not only generates the parables as a corpus, allowing us to see them as part of a continuity, a system of signs, but it also integrates

these proverbs into that system so that we can see them as inter-
related and expanded by the system.

BEATITUDES
(Luke 6:20b–23)

Beatitudes as a form also belong to the Wisdom tradition,[33] and
they are widespread in the synoptic tradition. Because the Beatitudes appear in both Matthew and Luke we will have to determine the most probable original form. Similarly, since beatitude is an established form in Wisdom literature, the nature of
the form itself must be considered.

Bultmann represents the consensus when he states that Luke
has preserved the more original version of the Q Beatitudes,
even though he cast the Beatitudes into the second person
plural.[34] Usually they occur in the third person. Jacques Dupont,
in an important study of Beatitudes, comes to the same conclusion, but on slightly different grounds. Though generally Beatitudes are formulated in the third person, it is by no means
universally so.[35] The telling point of Dupont's argument relies
upon a careful consideration of Beatitudes' construction. The
protasis of the Lucan Beatitudes does not specify second or third
person (although it normally is translated second person), and
specification comes only in the apodosis. The protasis easily
could be third person were it not for the apodosis. Dupont cites
evidence for all other Beatitudes having the specification in the
protasis.[36] The Lucan form is unique. For Dupont the first three
Beatitudes originally were in the third person.[37] The original form
would be translated as follows:

> Blessed (are) the poor,
>   for theirs is the Kingdom of God;
>
> Blessed (are) those who hunger now,
>   for they shall be satisfied;
>
> Blessed (are) those who weep now,
>   for they shall laugh.

In Wisdom literature "the form 'happy is the man . . .' expresses joy at some fulfillment of life, arrived at through the

fortunate outcome of some common situation."[38] G. Bertram has remarked that in the Old Testament "beatitude" always refers to persons and covers a wide spectrum of life: "It relates first to earthly blessings, a wife, children, beauty, earthly well-being, riches, honor, wisdom."[39] There was a close identification between secular and divine Wisdom.

Both Beardslee and F. Hauck stress that the Beatitudes preserved in the Q Sermon on the Plain have shifted from the common Wisdom tradition to an eschatological situation.[40] According to Beardslee the form Beatitude can adapt to this new situation because of "the old concern for the favorable outcome of a process."[41] The future impinges upon the present. Hauck maintains that the power of the Beatitudes "lies in their reversal of all human values,"[42] which he describes as "sacred paradoxes." This raises the question of just how and what kind of future is now present.

The structure of the three Beatitudes provides important clues as to their mutual interrelation. They have a protasis and apodosis, the construction of which is similar. The protasis includes an introductory adjective, "blessed" or "happy" (*makarioi*), followed by another adjective used substantively. In the first Beatitude the substantive is the adjective *ptochoi* (the poor), while the other two Beatitudes use present participles as substantives: "those who" is an English idiom for rendering a Greek participle. In the English translation the verb ("are") is supplied. "But the sense is not at all 'Blessed will be.' The present is secretly transformed by the future."[43] The following translation of the protasis of the following Beatitudes indicates the underlying Greek construction.

A	B	C	D
Blessed	(are)	the	Poor
Blessed	(are)	those who	Hunger

In the diagram the B term is supplied and the other terms are parallel. The construction of the apodosis is not as parallel. The apodosis for the last two Beatitudes is identical: the conjunction *hoti* (because) and a future tense verb. "They shall eat their full; they shall laugh." The English translation "they shall eat their full," represents one Greek word. But the apodosis of the first Beatitude is constructed differently: "Because theirs is the King- dom of God."[44] This translation has a one-to-one correspondence with the underlying Greek.

The first Beatitude's deviation in form suggests a route for the interpretation of Beatitudes as a group. Possession of the King- dom is a present reality in the first Beatitude, while the remedy for hunger and weeping lies in the future. This brings into sharp relief the difference between Kingdom and eating/laughter. The latter two are empirical in that they are observable—but the former, while no less real, is not observable in the same fash- ion. It is real and its present possession is somehow related to eating and laughing in the future. It guarantees that future re- versal. But in the Beatitudes, to designate those who are now poor, who hunger and weep as happy, clearly reverses and de- nies human standards, as Hauck points out.[45] As a group the three Beatitudes leave the hearer in a quandary: How can these be happy? How can the poor now possess the Kingdom? It is, of course, no less absurd to say that those who hunger *are* blessed because they *will* eat their full than to say that the poor *are* blessed because theirs *is* the Kingdom. In both instances a hearer must decide to abandon the normal understanding of Reality.

The underlying structure of these Beatitudes coheres with that of the parables. To describe as happy those who are not creates Illusion out of what is normally called Reality. Since the Beati- tude is Grace, the acceptance of Grace demands the renuncia- tion of Status—one must have no Status, i.e., be poor.

These Beatitudes generate an interesting surface tension be- tween the presence of Kingdom and futurity of relief for those who weep and hunger. This tension between an eschatology of already and not yet is derived at a deeper level from the interac- tion between the Comic and Tragic. In narrative parables this dynamic constrained the plot; here it expresses itself in the use of a temporal metaphor. That is, temporality must be under- stood metaphorically, not as a timetable for the Kingdom's arrival. As a symbol it cannot come, and yet because it is real it must be spoken of.

The temporal metaphor is ambivalent because within the Kingdom's symbolic structure Reality is Whole, not Divided. Expressed in temporal images Kingdom can be neither totally future nor totally present, for such an understanding would be dualistic. The contraries Reality as Whole–Reality as Divided demand that Kingdom's temporal metaphors express through ambiguity this unified version of Reality. The outcast's blessedness represents Kingdom's futurity.

KINGDOM SAYINGS

In a study of Jesus' understanding of Kingdom one normally begins with the so-called Kingdom sayings.[46] But as we argued in the first chapter, beginning with these sayings has led scholarship off course. One takes heart from Thomas S. Kuhn's *The Structure of Scientific Revolutions*, which shows that deviation from the standard method is often the first step in a new discovery.[47] We began with parables because they represent the most developed system of symbolic organization of Jesus' language, and we have pursued other *meshalim* as congenial to that symbol system. In the last part of this chapter we will turn our attention to Kingdom Sayings, the Lord's Prayer, and the Deeds of Jesus.

For the purposes of this analysis I have classified four proverbs as Kingdom Sayings, because Kingdom of God appears in them. For this reason our study of Kingdom Sayings will be divided into two groups: Proverbs and Dominical Sayings.

Proverbs (Luke 9:62; Mark 10:15, 23, 25)

Several features in these proverbs immediately attract our attention. All four proverbs use hyperbole, and the image of a child appears inappropriate. Such features appear regularly in proverbs. Child and rich are contraries, both of which are generated by the contraries Grace and Status. Their use coheres with the generative model for parables.

The first proverb raises certain problems. "No one who puts his hand to the plow and looks back is fit for the Kingdom of

God" (Luke 9:62). The word *euthetos* (fit) does not convey the sense of worthiness but rather of use.[48] The metaphor of plowing denotes what is of use for (or in) the Kingdom. But the vivid picture[49] of the plowman is disconcerting because it suggests single-mindedness and a certain striving. How does the plowman's activity compare with the farmer's passivity in the Seed Cast upon the Ground? Or should they be compared? In the parable, the farmer's passivity contrasts with the apocalyptic war in Joel, while in the proverb his single-mindedness in setting a furrow is hyperbole for "fitness" for Kingdom. Thus parable and proverb are not comparable, since they function differently. The plowman's single-mindedness results from Reality as Whole—he may not take time to calculate his path, to turn back, or let go of the plow. Thus the image coheres with the general theme that Reality is not dualistic.

These proverbs refer to Kingdom as something to "be fit for," to "receive," and to "enter."[50] Norman Perrin remarks that one cannot literally do these things to a symbol; one can only respond to its evocative power.[51] Perrin, of course, quite correctly calls our attention to this unusual usage. But in one sense he misses the mark, because one can enter a symbol, since "enter" is itself symbolic language. The inappropriateness of "Kingdom" as a translation for *malkuth* is what leads astray. Gustaf Dalman demonstrated this at the beginning of the century: in Judaism *malkuth* refers to God's "kingly rule," never "Kingdom." It demonstrates his sovereignty, not his territory.[52] So the question is more appropriately phrased, how does one become fit for, receive, or enter into God's ruling activity? The plowman's single-mindedness determines whether one is fit for the ruling activity of Yahweh. In proverb, "to receive" and "to enter" are correlated. The verbs heighten the symbolism of the proverbs and their referent Kingdom because they are so incongruous. Rhetorically the tension is concentrated in the proverb to destroy the hearer's Illusion and Ideology about Kingdom.

Dominical Sayings (Luke 11:20, 17:20–21; Matthew 11:12)

These three sayings about Kingdom have all been the subject of extensive debate and exegesis.[53] Since our concern is to determine whether their underlying structure coheres with that of the parables, we will refer to the exegetical controversy only where significant unresolved problems exist.

Luke 11:20

The first saying, cast as a conditional sentence, has its *Sitz im Leben* in the debate over Jesus' activity as an exorcist.[54] This is an important link between the sayings tradition and Jesus' deeds, a topic to be considered later.

In recent years the saying has been used as an unambiguous example of the Kingdom being present.[55] The verb of the apodosis (*ephthasen*) in the aorist tense means "has come."[56] While this remains beyond dispute, Perrin in his last study of the saying warned against understanding the saying in temporal terms.[57] Having decided that Kingdom is present, or proclaimed as present by Jesus, critics assume that their task is over without reflecting on the absurdity or paradoxical character of the statement. What does it mean to say the Kingdom has come? What does it say about Kingdom or presence? Is it significant that the saying is conditional? Because it has been read as part of the debate over the eschatology of Jesus, its resonance has been silenced. As a way beyond that debate, we will turn our attention to the saying's diachronic heritage and its structure as a conditional clause.

Kümmel, in discussing the parallel saying at Matt. 12:28, sees no convincing argument by which to decide whether "by the Spirit of God" (Matthew) or "by the finger of God" (Luke) is more original.[58] For him the Lucan text is probably original, because Luke would have preferred a saying dealing with the Spirit. But at any rate the difference is "inessential." Perrin, on the other hand, adopting the same argument for Luke's originality, maintains that the difference between Matthew and Luke is very important.[59] He sees "finger of God" as a reference to Exod. 8:15, which narrates the third plague. When Aaron strikes the dust, a great swarm of gnats appears "on man and beast." The magicians of Egypt, unable to duplicate the feat, reply to Pharaoh, "This is the finger of God."[60] Perrin also quotes a text from Midr. Exod. Rab. 10.7 that interprets this saying: "When the magicians saw that they could not produce the lice, they recognized immediately that the happenings (the plagues) were the work of God and not the work of demons."[61] He concludes beyond doubt that the saying claims that exorcisms are the eschatological activity of God.[62]

I find Perrin's argument convincing. But the reference's depth in the diachronic tradition is deeper than he suspects. Finger of God is also used in Exod. 31:18 and the parallel Deut. 9:10 to describe God's writing upon the tablet of the Law. This reinforces finger of God as an expression associated with the decisive intervention by God into human existence. Finally, Perrin has overlooked the context of Exod. 8:15. Following the magicians' report that the plague is the finger of God, the text continues, "But Pharaoh's heart was hardened, and he would not listen to them as the Lord has said." In Jesus' saying finger of God is not only an appeal to recognize God's wonder working present in exorcism, but also an implicit rebuke to the audience for their hardness of hearts. The saying casts them on the side of Pharaoh.

Furthermore, the saying is a conditional sentence whose protasis uses *ei* (if) with the indicative, indicating that "the condition is considered a real case."[63] But this creates acute problems for interpreting the saying: Which component is real? While from the audience's viewpoint the only undebated assumption is the casting out of demons, there are four possibilities in the sentence: The Finger of God / Casting out of demons / Has come / Kingdom of God. The four terms' interrelation creates tension in the saying. First, the hearer must decide if the demons are cast out by the finger of God. The saying does not argue that because "I" cast out demons therefore "I" do it by God's power.[64] Rather, since it is conditional the hearer decides. The condition poses the question of the Real: is this the finger of God? The debate is not over the casting out of demons, but the claim implied in finger of God.

Finger of God and Kingdom of God also interact. Kingdom symbolically conjures up Israel's past wherein God acted as King. Surely the contest with Pharaoh involves the myth of Yahweh's kingship. By alluding to that event, the text makes a very specific reference to God as King: in Jesus' exorcisms the power of God that conquered Pharaoh is now at work. This creates a dilemma for the audience. If they reject the exorcism as the finger of God, they side with Pharaoh; on the other hand, is the casting out of a few demons any real evidence for the presence of Kingdom? Are these exorcisms to be compared with the plagues of Egypt? If they do equate the casting out of demons with the finger of God, then the Kingdom has arrived.[65] Its presence or non-presence is dependent upon the acceptance of the condition as real.

The language of the saying is similar in structure to the parables and proverbs. Because it is conditional, it demands Faith on the part of the hearer. In our generative model Faith's contrary is Ideology, which is implied when the hearer is asked to abandon the Ideology of Kingdom as future and accept it as already present. The audience must see God's action with Pharaoh not as past but as present. Faith exposes its opposite, Reality as Divided. In this saying Reality is represented by an implicit temporal metaphor.

finger of God	exorcism	Kingdom of God
past	present	future

These three terms have temporal equivalents which are collapsed in the saying, or, as our generative model indicates, Faith implies Reality as Whole. If the hearer can accept that the same finger of God that was active against Pharaoh is now active in Jesus' exorcisms, then the Kingdom of God has come.

Luke 17:20–21

Our second Kingdom saying has had a long history of interpretation. For example, at the turn of the century, Adolf von Harnack used the text to uphold his interpretation of the Kingdom as a "spiritual," interior reality. He understood the ambiguous Greek phrase, *entos hymōn*, as "within you."[66]

Even today the translation and exact meaning of the phrase *entos hymōn* remains central. Should it be translated "within you" or "in your midst"? The debate revolves around three separate considerations: (1) the meaning of the Greek phrase in normal usage; (2) possible Aramaic equivalents; (3) the contextual, synchronic meaning of the saying. Each of these problems will be considered separately.

Investigations into Greek usage have proven inconclusive, since the word *entos* can mean either "among" or "within."[67] In its only other occurrence in the New Testament, *entos* definitely has the meaning of "within."[68] The inability to solve the problem on the basis of Greek word study has led to a search for an Aramaic background. This too has proven inconclusive, since there is no Aramaic preposition with a similar, ambiguous meaning.[69] The ambiguity may predate Luke, as an examination of the Thomas tradition indicates. An interesting parallel to Luke 17:20–21 occurs in Thomas 3.

> Jesus said: "If those who lead you say to you: 'See, the Kingdom is in heaven,' then the birds of the heaven will precede you. If they say to you: 'It is in the sea,' then the fish will precede you. But the Kingdom is within you and it is without you. If you will know yourselves, then you will be known and you will know that you are the sons of the Living Father. But if you do not know yourselves, then you are in poverty and you are poverty."

In this saying the "Lo, here; lo, there" is developed into particular examples, but the phrase that concerns us remains: "The Kingdom is within you and without you." Further, in a series of fragments of a Greek Gospel of Thomas in the Oxyrhynchus Papyrus, the preposition used is *entos*.[70] This indicates that the ambiguity over the meaning of *entos* is deep within the sayings tradition.

The inability to determine the preposition's meaning has led to attempts to analyze the context. Kümmel argues that *entos* must be understood as contrasted to "not coming with signs to be observed," and the denial of pointing here or there.[71] The Greek meaning of "signs to be observed" (*meta paratērēseōs*) is "observation especially of premonitory signs and symptoms." According to Kümmel the saying denies that the future coming of the Kingdom can be observed with definite signs.[72] "Neither here nor there" rejects any attempt to speculate on the Kingdom's place. Kümmel concludes: "So the desire to calculate the date of the Kingdom of God and the search for it are rejected in two different forms; for neither the time nor the place of its coming can be recognized if it is thus wrongly sought."[73] If, then, Kingdom were to be "within you," it would have to have "a quality of inwardness." But this can be rejected because "to calculate the Kingdom of God in advance or to search for it in the future can hardly be contrasted with 'in you' as a matter of a place, but only as one of time."[74] Perrin adds to Kümmel's argument the observation that such an interior understanding of Kingdom would be without precedent in Jesus' teaching.[75] Thus by process of elimination Kümmel concludes that *entos* must be translated "among."

The debate over the translation of *entos* demonstrates what misdirections occur in asking the wrong questions. "Within you" is rejected both because of its association with an outdated liberal theology and because of the dominance of an apocalyptic understanding of Kingdom. But must there be a choice between "within" and "among"? Could not the ambiguous preposition be there because it is ambiguous? Both Thomas and Luke have indicated the antiquity of that ambiguity. Scholarship has misappropriated this saying by using it to answer a question it originally never intended to answer.

Closer attention to the saying's structure confirms this observation. It is divided into three parts, two negative and one positive. The following translation–diagram reflects the careful structuring of the Greek text.

not is coming   the Kingdom of God
                                                          with observation

nor will they say

                       Behold here or there
                       Behold for   the Kingdom of God
                                                      entos hymōn is

There is a phonetic parallelism between the initial words of the two negative phrases, as well as a clear pattern of organization by the doublets *ou* (not), *idou* (behold).[76] "With observation"

(*meta paratērēseōs*) parallels *entos hymōn*. The saying consists of
two contrasting sets:

is coming, will say − − − − − − − − − − is (*estin*)
with observation, here or there − − − *entos hymōn*

A temporal contrast between future and present sets up the
second. If the Kingdom is not future but present, where is it?
"Not with observation" indicates that Kingdom does not exhibit
extraordinary signs, and "not here nor there" confirms that an
empirical location is a misjudgment. But if this is so, what is it?
Entos hymōn—the ambiguous phrase is paradoxical; the two
negatives expect literal answers. The saying throws the hearer
into confusion because it destroys criteria for judgment, demand-
ing instead an insight into Kingdom.

The surface use of negatives in the saying is constrained by
the negative contraries of the generative model. While agreeing
with Perrin that "not with observation" signifies a rejection of an
apocalyptic view of history, the surface expression partakes of a
larger complex represented by Ideology. The contrary, Reality
as Divided, generates "neither here nor there." The saying's
paradoxical ending leads the hearer to the other pole of the
model by suggesting that what was accepted as Reality is Illusion. To accept the paradox of *entos hymōn* as a description of
Kingdom grants one the experience of Reality. But Reality demands the rejection of Ideology and Reality as Divided. Surrender of Ideology leads to its opposite, the experience of Reality as
Whole—surrender of the Kingdom's future expectation and the
acknowledgment of its presence. But to so surrender, the hearer
must have Faith that the Ideological Reality by which one had
navigated is Illusion and that its rejection has led to Reality.
Thus the surface structure of this saying is generated by a series
of complex interrelations between the terms of the generative
model.

Matthew 11:12

In our final Kingdom saying, the central problem turns on the
interpretation of the verb *biazetai*, normally translated "has suf-

fered violence." The controversy over the verb's translation grants easy entrance into the problems connected with the saying.

The form of the verb *biazetai* can be either middle deponent or passive voice. This grammatical difference vitally affects the saying's meaning. If the verb is middle voice then it would be translated "the Kingdom of God is breaking in with violence"; if passive, it would be "the Kingdom of God is suffering violence."

The classical discussion of the grammar comes from Gottlob Schrenk.[77] He begins by showing that the verb refers to forced action as contrasted with voluntary action. It has a sense of "to force, to compel, to overpower" (sometimes militarily and sometimes sexually). The accent falls upon a negative connotation of force. Schrenk then presents the possibilities for translating Matt. 11:12. Although he notes that the middle sense is the normal one in Greek,[78] in this text he argues it is very difficult. The phrase, "violent men attack it" in the second part of the saying, "is most naturally construed as an interpretation of the first part of the statement." That is, violent men are the ones who are doing violence to Kingdom. This demands a passive verb. Also the middle sense "is completely out of keeping with the conception of the *Basileia* (Kingdom) in the Synoptics." For these two reasons Schrenk "has shown that *biazetai* must be taken as a passive."[79] But I find the arguments less than compelling. First, the uncontested rarity of the passive means the middle must be preferred only if it can be shown to be impossible (not merely difficult).[80] Second, the phrase "violent men attack it" need not be understood as explaining *biazetai*, but either in contrast or parallel.[81] And finally the middle is not incompatible with Jesus' symbol, Kingdom.

A strong argument for *biazetai* as a middle has been offered by Otto Betz in an article entitled "The Eschatological Interpretation of the Sinai-Tradition in Qumran and the New Testament."[82] He understands the saying against the background of Exod. 19:24, which is part of the giving of the Law at Sinai, a scene that Betz argues engages the theme of Yahweh's kingship.[83] The text is one of a number connected with Sinai that express the history of religions' notion of the sacred boundary. This envisions a wall or boundary around the sacred which protects the people from possible harm from exposure to the sacred.[84] The Exodus text also is of interest because *biazetai* is used in the Septuagint. "Do not let the priest and people break through (*biazethosan*) to come up to God lest the Lord destroy (*apolesēi*) them."

Betz does not completely make a case because he exhibits no texts where God breaks out in the precise fashion demanded of a middle in Matt. 11:12. In the Exodus text God does not break out, but the priest and people are warned not to break out. Betz is nevertheless correct because he has recalled for us that sacred power is not always beneficent, as Rudolf Otto demonstrated, but can be negative as well. In the Exodus text, the Septuagint understood that for the people or priest to approach God at Sinai was dangerous, for he might destroy them.[85] In Jesus' saying the divine power of God is not only circumscribed by a boundary, but is breaking out. And that breaking out is violent, a moment of danger: "The Kingdom of God is breaking out by force."

A middle sense for *biazetai* also coheres with the saying's structure. "Violent men" does not describe who "is breaking out" but represents a counterforce to the Kingdom's violent outbreak. Their intent is clear: to plunder, to seize, to carry away (*harpazousin*). To question the identity of the violent is to move beyond the license of the saying. Finally, the Kingdom breaking out with violence is not contrary to Jesus' language. Anyone who can compare Kingdom to Leaven, can speak of Kingdom breaking out with violent force. This is another example of Jesus' use of inappropriate images to describe Kingdom. Kingdom is not simply a common event, but it partakes of tragedy and inflicts tragedy.

The debate over *biazetai* unfortunately has obscured other dimensions of the saying. It announces that the Kingdom and men have been engaged in violent conflict from the days of John the Baptist. Ernst Käsemann remarked that with this saying Jesus designates John the Baptist's ministry as inaugurating a new aeon.[86] In his interpretation the apocalyptic assumption has reduced Kingdom to a cipher for new age. As a timetable, the saying no longer provokes scandal, because evidence for the Kingdom's coming is overlooked for its final coming is in the future. But as we have argued throughout, Kingdom is not equivalent to new aeon. As a symbol it is polyvalent and therefore much more elusive. In this saying Jesus demarks its violent intrusion as historical, "since the days of John the Baptist." Because the saying is part of a Sinai interpretation trajectory (Betz), it implicitly relates the outbreaking to Sinai. Many authors, in rejecting a middle sense for *biazetai*, contend that Jesus interpreted his exorcisms in the context of a holy war. And surely part of the Kingdom's violence finds expression in the exorcisms, as the saying about "the finger of God" proves. But this only exacerbates the real scandal. Is the present outbreaking to be compared to God's ruling activity at Sinai? The saying resembles both the Mustard Plant and Leaven. The Kingdom engaging in violent attack is as inappropriate as leaven, while the *evidence* for the outbreak is more in line with Mustard Plant than the Great Tree.

In stating that Kingdom is an historical phenomenon, attacking and being attacked since the time of John the Baptist, the saying implies a rejection of Reality as Divided. The Kingdom as already here, as presently acting, sees Reality as Whole, even though at war. The contraries Reality as Whole–Reality as Divided constrain the double motion of the saying. In the generative model Reality as Divided implies The Comic or The Tragic with its contrary, Comedy through Tragedy. By breaking into history and becoming historical, Kingdom must engage in tragic possibility or else it will be a simple comic reality. To be Kingdom, to provide a comic possibility, it must appear as tragic, that is, as attacking. The boundary protecting the dangerous sacred must be destroyed because Kingdom demands wholeness, but it creates wholeness in violence.

THE LORD'S PRAYER

As a final example of Jesus' language we will consider the Lord's Prayer. Our concern will be the prayer's orientation and especially its second petition, an unambiguous expression of Kingdom as future: "Thy Kingdom come."

In reconstructing Jesus' eschatology the problem is the confusion of Kingdom as symbol with an apocalyptic image of the new aeon. When parables are interpreted from the viewpoint of a timetable of the new aeon, for example in the so-called parables of growth, parable as metaphor is forfeited. Parables assert that God's ruling activity is present, and with the proverbs (and the other sayings we have examined) they attempt to shock or coerce the hearer into an experience of Kingdom. How then is the Lord's Prayer to be understood in light of our previous analysis?

Joachim Jeremias's suggested reconstruction of an original form can be taken as a starting point.[87]

> Dear Father,
> Hallowed be thy name
> Thy kingdom come
> Our bread for tomorrow/give us today
> And forgive us our debts/as we also herewith
>   forgive our debtors
> And let us not succumb to the temptation.

The parallelism between this prayer and the *Kaddish*, the traditional Jewish synagogue prayer, has been noted by a number of commentators.

> Magnified and sanctified be his great name in the world that he has created according to his will. May he establish his kingdom in your lifetime and in your days and in the lifetime of all the house of Israel, even speedily and at a near time.

While one normally contrasts the *Kaddish*'s verbosity with the simplicity of the Lord's Prayer,[88] such an observation only accounts for the difference in context—the formal, liturgical *Kaddish* and the spontaneous Lord's Prayer. The Lord's Prayer itself becomes verbose as it is handed on, even to the point of taking on a title, "The Lord's Prayer."

The prayer's invocation has provoked a separate debate. Jeremias maintains that behind the Greek *pater* of Luke is an Aramaic expression *Abba*, which for him designates Jesus' special and customary manner of addressing God.[89] Hans Conzelmann, among others, sees Paul's use of *Abba* in Gal. 4:6 and Rom. 8:15 as an indication of ecclesiastical formulation.[90] For our purposes we do not need a resolution of the debate. One need not agree with Jeremias that *Abba* was Jesus' customary address of God (the evidence does not really support that); nor must one agree with Conzelmann that its use by the early church means it cannot have been used by Jesus. The negative criterion cannot indicate what Jesus did *not* say, but only what he could have said. Our concern is with the usage in this prayer, and there appears to be no good reason to reject the authenticity of Jeremias's reconstruction.[91]

In Aramaic *Abba* is the child's word for father, equivalent to the English "daddy." As an invocation it burlesques formal invocations, an irreverence that Matthew's tradition remedies with the proper liturgical invocation, "Our Father who art in heaven." *Abba*'s poking fun at formalism has been overlooked in the past, but such language is typical of Jesus. Just as Mustard Plant burlesques Great Tree, so *Abba* burlesques a formal, solemn approach to God. The invocation is a shock to the everyday way of prayer, and it is therefore generated by the contraries Reality–Illusion.

But precisely because *Abba* imaginatively conjures up childhood feelings of intimacy and dependency, for those who so address God the immense distance between God and themselves has collapsed. That is, they see Reality as Whole, not as Divided. Eschatology is realized; for them the Kingdom has come. Furthermore the use of the child's *Abba* destroys the Status of God's formal title, indicating that *Abba* is a title of Grace.

The prayer's first petition parallels the *Kaddish*. "To make holy," in Hebrew, *qādash*, is to set apart. The petition belongs to the same tradition of sayings as Matt. 11:12: To hallow is to set up the sacred boundary, to denote where God is. The setting apart of his name will invoke a healing wherein all will be drawn into the intimacy of *Abba*. At first glance, the petition to hallow or set apart appears to understand Reality as Divided, which would be unique in Jesus' language. But the name to be set apart is *Abba*, which connotes Reality as Whole, Status as destroyed. This transforms "hallow" so that the setting apart of such a name encompasses all within it—Reality becomes divisionless as it returns to its childhood, to when God is *Abba*.

The second petition is an unambiguous reference to the Kingdom as future: thy Kingdom come. Once again the petition is patterned upon the *Kaddish* with "come," normal in the Jesus tradition, replacing the expected "establish." But the coming of a Kingdom is quite different from its establishment. The incongruity of a Kingdom coming heightens the language's tensive symbolism. Formally as a prayer of petition patterned on the *Kaddish*, the petition could hardly be anything other than future. But in what sense is it to come? Norman Perrin has pointed out two options. Because *Abba* symbolizes for the petitioners that Kingdom has come, they pray either that others may experience its coming or they are praying in its present experience for its future fulfillment. Of the two options, Perrin chooses the latter because it coheres with the eschatology of parables and the prayer's personal nature rules out a corporate understanding.[92]

But is it an either/or choice? The prayer calls for the Kingdom's present experience to be consummated by granting to others the experience of its coming. Since the coming involves the appearance of Reality, it also involves its contrary Illusion. Within the terms of the generative model, Reality's final coming means that those living under the Illusion that the Kingdom has not been established will realize that in Reality it has come.

For Perrin the first option is jarring with the prayer's personal nature, although what he means by personal is not clear. If it means the intimacy implied in *Abba*, then why is the request for others to experience that so jarring? But if personal equals individualistic[93] then Perrin has misinterpreted the prayer, since it gives no indication of being individualistic: all the pronouns referring to people are plural. Furthermore, if Kingdom is a symbol for Israel's experience of God as King, how can it be individualistic? What would be more natural than for a group of Jews to pray that all their people may experience *Abba* in the Kingdom's coming?

Finally, Perrin argues that the first option must be rejected because it does not cohere with the parables. For him the Parables of Growth signal a future consummation, but, as we have argued, such an understanding asks the wrong question of those parables. The petition, within its context, does cohere with the parable's underlying structure. Perrin's either/or is a both. The petition requests both that others may experience the coming of the Kingdom and that the Kingdom come—that all may experience God as *Abba*; that Reality may dispel the Illusion surrounding it; that the Kingdom of God break out of its boundary.

The two "our" petitions confirm the analysis of the second petition's interaction with the first part of the prayer. While these petitions are somewhat difficult in their reconstruction,[94] they both have the same structural pattern. The first one requests that the future be present now, while the second confirms the mutual interrelation of having been forgiven debts and the forgiving of others' debts. In the first petition the future collapses into the present, i.e., Kingdom is not Reality as Divided but Reality as Whole expressed as a temporal metaphor. The second petition demonstrates both the prayer's corporate nature and its orientation toward those outside the community of those who say *Abba*. The petitioner's ability to forgive every debt owed is the expression of one's own having been forgiven. A Reality as Divided into debtors and creditors is a Reality that implies Status and is therefore the opposite of Kingdom, a moment of Grace.

The prayer ends with a request that the petitioner not be allowed to fail at the time of the great test.[95] This request is related to Matt. 11:12. It warns that the Kingdom's coming is a time of violence and danger. The contraries, Comedy through Tragedy—Comic or Tragic, generate this petition. It is the petitioner's acknowledgment of the inevitable confrontation with Tragedy in the forgiveness of debts, in the coming of the Kingdom, in the setting apart of the name, in the audacity of "daddy."

DEEDS

An examination of Jesus' activities remains a neglected area of research. The reasons for this are understandable. The way the tradition developed works against such an analysis, since prior to the composition of the synoptic Gospels the tradition was oral, made up of mostly independent, isolated sayings. The form of preservation was either logia (sayings) or narrative. The recovery of actions became difficult since they will always be embedded in a narrative form. We never attain the direct immediacy of the logia in a gospel narrative.

The accounts of Jesus' Baptism, the Cleansing of the Temple, or the Entrance into Jerusalem undoubtedly derive from actual events. The negative criterion indicates high probability, since the events behind the narratives are not likely to have been invented by the early church because of potentially embarrassing features. Jesus' baptism presents christological problems, and the Cleansing and Entrance into Jerusalem have political implications. But the actions remain unavailable to us because we have no way of ascertaining how Jesus understood them. As narratives cast in the third person, their point of view is different. Storytelling interests and the early church's apologetic needs have so clothed them that their original significance is difficult to know.[96] Does the Baptism, for example, represent the moment of conversion that consolidated Jesus' experience of the Kingdom of God, the experience that generated the entire phenomenon we have been examining, the moment that gave rise to the structure of World we have examined? Does his entrance into Jerusalem on an ass represent a burlesque of Messianic expectations—a pointing to the Illusion of expected grandeur? Is the Cleansing of the Temple an attack upon Reality as Divided into Temple and non-Temple, parallel to his attack on clean and unclean? Is he destroying the Status of a place? One seems reduced to speculation because there is no way methodologically to verify an answer to these questions. The narratives which have surrounded these events are not interested in answering our questions.

The narratives of Jesus' exorcisms and healings are a variation on these same methodological problems. The stereotype's form prevents a determination of the event's history.[97] Even if particular exorcisms and healings attributed to Jesus are authentic, what gain has been made?[98] Surely the narratives are typical of what happened; that after all is one of a form's purposes. That Jesus was a wonder worker needs to be insisted upon;[99] but the

miracle stories only provide us with the early community's interpretation of those events. As we saw above, the sayings grant an
entrance into Jesus' interpretation. From our point of view
Jesus' exorcisms in their very ordinariness confront and jar the
audience's Reality. His claim that they are "the finger of God" is
an interpretation in line with his linguistic usage.

One characteristic deed of Jesus escapes some of these methodological problems because it carries its own implied interpretation: Jesus' association with the outcast. It might indeed be
termed a symbolic action. His normal companions include publicans and sinners,[100] prostitutes, lepers, the *'am ha-aretz*.[101] While
individual sayings dealing with Jesus' association are hard to
authenticate by means of the negative criterion,[102] nevertheless the
symbolic structure of Jesus' World would lead one to expect
such an association.[103] In light of the contraries Reality as Whole–
Reality as Divided, exclusion of the outcast would have violated
the basic model.

But the question is even more difficult than it seems. While
including the outcast in the Kingdom (Luke 6:20), Jesus does
not demand that the publicans renounce their profession[104] and he
goes on to identify himself with them (Matt. 11:19). A zealot
would reject the publican out of hand and the Pharisee would
try to convert him to the correct observance of Torah. But Jesus'
course differs—the outcast are his consorts.[105] His association with
the outcast is a cause of scandal.[106] This dimension of his behavior
goes beyond the simple offer of repentance. The "going beyond"
is generated by the same symbolic demand that in other instances has generated hyperbole, paradox, and the inappropriate
in his language. The conflict between the Reality of Kingdom
and the Illusion of the Accepted generates this "excess." His
association with the outcast represents Reality as Whole while at
the same time exposing his opponents as captive to Illusion. Is it
any wonder that from their point of view his construct of a
counter-world is demonic?

But Jesus' siding with the outcast raises the question of his
relation to "established Judaism."[107] Although the tradition accentuates the conflict with the Pharisees, nevertheless the animosity
between Jesus and the Pharisees is undoubtedly historical. If

they are excluded from the Kingdom as a group, does this sig-
nify that Jesus himself viewed Reality as Divided? But the Pharisees are themselves a symbol of "the establishment." They have
a vested interest in Status and Reality as Divided.[108] Given the organization of Jesus' symbolic World, their opposition is understandable. In one sense the position of established Judaism demands the position of Jesus and vice versa. They and Jesus are
locked in an attempt to articulate symbolically Israel's experience
of Yahweh as King. There is no language of Jesus without the
debate over Israel's heritage.[109]

We have seen that Jesus' language coheres, that different
forms exhibit the same characteristics. His language is World-
shattering, in some cases form-shattering. And yet at the same
time it is new-World-affirmative. This leads us to reexamine
both the presiding symbol of this language and its outcome.

NOTES

1. *Jesus and the Language of the Kingdom* (Philadelphia: Fortress
Press, 1976), p. 41, besides the parables he gives the following list as
the minimum that would receive consensus as authentic. Luke 11:20;
17:20–21; Matt. 11:12; Luke 11:2–4; Mark 3:27; 3:24–26; 8:35; Luke
9:62; Mark 10:23b, 25; Luke 9:60a; Matt. 7:13–14; Mark 10:31; 7:15;
10:15; Luke 14:11; 16:15; Matt. 5:39b–41; 5:44–48.

2. Norman Perrin, *Rediscovering the Teaching of Jesus* (New York:
Harper and Row, 1967), p. 39. For Perrin "that which is most characteristic of Jesus . . . will be found not in the things which he shares
with his contemporaries, but in the things wherein he differs from
them." This is an extreme statement which surely was not meant literally. One is reminded of Alfred Loisy's biting remarks against Harnack's similar attempt to find the essence of Jesus. "There would be
little logic in taking for the whole essence of one religion the points
that differentiate it from another. The monotheistic faith is common
to Judaism, Christianity, and Mahometanism; but we are not
therefore to conclude that the essential features of these three religions
must be sought apart from the monotheistic conception" (*The Gospel
and the Church*, trans. Christopher Home, ed. Bernard Scott, Lives of
Jesus Series [1903; Philadelphia: Fortress Press, 1976], p. 9).

3. A *Future for the Historical Jesus* (1971; reprint ed., Philadelphia: Fortress Press, 1981), pp. 33–35, Keck's warning is apropos, but he does not develop a clear methodology for dealing with the gray areas, those points in common between Jesus, contemporary Judaism, and the early Christian communities.

4. Perrin, *Rediscovering*, p. 102, refers to Jesus' table fellowship with tax collectors and sinners as an "acted parable." While indicating an important characteristic of the practice, this reduces an action to a word.

5. *An Introduction to the New Hermeneutic* (Philadelphia: Westminster Press, 1969), p. 152.

6. In view of the continuing and developing debate on this issue, my discussion will be most tentative and limited.

7. Hans Conzelmann, *Jesus*, trans. Raymond Lord, intro. John Reumann (Philadelphia: Fortress Press, 1973), p. iii. Even Crossan used Heidegger's categories to arrange his three groups of parables (*In Parables* [New York: Harper and Row, 1973]).

8. William A. Beardslee, *Literary Criticism of the New Testament*, Guides to Biblical Scholarship (Philadelphia: Fortress Press, 1970), p. 31; "Uses of the Proverbs in the Synoptic Gospels," *Interpretation* 24 (1970): 65ff.

9. Lonergan, *Method in Theology* (New York: Herder and Herder, 1972), p. 213, makes a similar point. Because a proverb is non-systematic, it is subject to the revision of critical thought; but insight still remains primary.

10. "Uses of Proverbs," p. 69.

11. Ibid., p. 64.

12. Beardslee's term (*Literary Criticism*, p. 32).

13. "Uses of Proverbs," p. 71. Perrin makes a strong case for accepting the authenticity of the proverbs (*Jesus and the Language*, p. 50).

14. Ibid., p. 69.

15. Ibid., p. 67.

16. Ibid., p. 68.

17. Perrin, *Jesus and the Language*, pp. 51ff., does not appreciate the scale, e.g., he has a group called "the most radical sayings," of which he gives two examples (one does not fit on Beardslee's grouping as radical, the other does not appear at all). Perrin's classifications are not helpful since they are derived from a variety of different sources.

18. In this discussion of proverbs, as has been our procedure, there is no attempt to be exhaustive. My selection is not always identical with that of Beardslee.

19. Rudolf Bultmann, *History of the Synoptic Tradition*, hereinafter *HST*, trans. John Marsh (New York: Harper and Row, 1963), p. 74–75.

20. *Jesus and the Language*, p. 53.

21. Perrin, ibid., p. 52, classifies this proverb under the rubric "eschatological reversal," and remarks that this is one of the best attested features of Jesus' language. This may be true, but I would suggest that eschatological reversal is generated by a deeper organization of images represented by our model.

22. Perrin, *Rediscovering*, p. 140, and *Jesus and the Language*, p. 53.

23. Eduard Schweizer, *The Good News According to Mark*, trans. Donald H. Madvig (Richmond: John Knox Press, 1970), p. 86.

24. This performance is very much like the Leaven.

25. *Jesus and the Language*, p. 53.

26. Beardslee, *Literary Criticism*, pp. 32–33.

27. Contra Perrin (*Rediscovering*, p. 147), "If we may accept the axiom that Jesus knew what he was talking about, then we must recognize that these are not specific commandments and that they were never meant to be taken literally. What we have here are illustrations of a principle." Robert C. Tannehill, *The Sword of His Mouth*, Semeia Studies (Missoula, Mont.: Scholars Press and Philadelphia: Fortress Press, 1975), pp. 88–101, correctly accents the imaginative impact of the sayings.

28. Perrin, ibid., p. 149. Joachim Jeremias, *New Testament Theology: The Proclamation of Jesus*, trans. John Bowden (New York: Charles Scribner's Sons, 1971), pp. 141 and 210 minimizes the attack upon sins of the tongue.

29. *Rediscovering*, p. 150.

30. To see the distinction between the secular and religious as a fundamental distinction of Jewish religion is an extreme statement. Neither Judaism nor Jesus radically identifies Yahweh with either nature or culture; on the other hand, Judaism's affirmation that Yahweh has made them a holy nation does seem to move toward bridging the gap.

31. For a reconstruction of this saying cf. Bultmann, *HST*, p. 79.

32. John Dominic Crossan, *Raid on the Articulate: Comic Eschatology in Jesus and Borges* (New York: Harper and Row, 1976), p. 65, accentuates the parody of these sayings.

33. Beardslee, *Literary Criticism*, p. 36, sees Beatitudes as a specialized form of the proverb. Bultmann, *HST*, p. 72, lists Blessings in general as logia (proverbs) but deals with the Beatitudes as prophetic

sayings, pp. 109ff. G. Bertram and F. Hauck, *"Makarios," Theological Dictionary of the New Testament*, hereinafter *TDNT*, ed. Gerhard Kittel, trans. Geoffrey Bromiley (Grand Rapids: Eerdmans, 1968), 4:364, classify beatitude as a wisdom form.

34. *HST*, pp. 109–10. Georg Strecker, "Die Antithesen der Berg-predigt," *Zeitschrift für die neutestamentliche Wissenschaft* 69 (1978): 36–72, has challenged this but is not convincing.

35. *Les Béatitudes* (Louvain: E. Nauwelaerts, 1958), 1: 279. The evidence for the second-person form is given on pp. 275–79. Chap. 8 is a very thorough discussion of the Lucan form of the Beatitudes.

36. Ibid., p. 281; even in the long beatitude of v. 22, *este*, "you (pl.) are," is used in the protasis. For a summary of Dupont's argument see p. 297.

37. The argument of Ernst Käsemann, "The Beginnings of Christian Theology," in *New Testament Questions of Today*, trans. W. J. Montague (Philadelphia: Fortress Press, 1969), pp. 100–101, that the Beatitudes are the formulation of Christian prophets is to be rejected; cf. Bultmann, *HST*, p. 378.

38. Beardslee, *Literary Criticism*, p. 36.

39. *"Makarios,"* p. 365.

40. Beardslee, *Literary Criticism*, p. 37; Hauck, *"Makarios,"* p. 365. R. A. Guelich, "The Matthean Beatitudes: 'Entrance Requirements' or Eschatological Blessing?" *Journal of Biblical Literature*, hereinafter *JBL*, 95 (1976): 415–34.

41. Beardslee, ibid. He further argues that the eschatological proverb at Rev. 14:13 is "in the process of transformation into a revealer speech in which a divine mystery is disclosed." In the example from Revelation this is appropriate since the speaker is a voice from heaven.

42. Hauck, *"Makarios,"* p. 368. Richard A. Edwards, *A Theology of Q* (Philadelphia: Fortress Press, 1976), p. 62, remarks that "The contrast between the now and the then implies that the present world's criteria of worth will be overthrown."

43. Beardslee, *Literary Criticism*, p. 38.

44. In comparison with Matthew's form, it would appear that Q did not have the present tense of the verb "to be," i.e., the original form would be similar to the apodosis of Matthew's version of this Beatitude.

45. Hauck, *"Makarios,"* p. 368; cf. Beardslee, *Literary Criticism*, p. 38: "Indeed these sayings can be used as a pointed reversal of popular standards which valued strength, self-assertiveness, and prudence rather than the stance of the beatitudes."

46. E.g., Perrin, *Jesus and the Language*.

47. Second edition (Chicago: University of Chicago Press, 1970), esp. pp. 85ff.

48. Walter Bauer, *A Greek-English Lexicon of the New Testament,* hereinafter *BAG,* trans. William Arndt and Wilbur Gingrich, 2d rev. ed. by Gingrich and Frederick W. Danker (Chicago: University of Chicago Press, 1979), p. 320. Cf. Luke 14:34–35.

49. Joachim Jeremias, *Parables of Jesus,* trans. H. S. Hooke (New York: Charles Scribner's Sons, 1963), p. 195, offers a vivid description of the process: "The very light Palestinian plough is guided with one hand. This one hand, generally the left, must at the same time keep the plough upright, regulate its depth by pressure, and lift it over the rocks and stones in its path. The ploughman uses the other hand to drive the unruly oxen with a goad about two yards long, fitted with an iron spike. At the same time he must continually look between the hindquarters of the oxen, keeping the furrow in sight. This primitive kind of plough needs dexterity and concentrated attention. If the ploughman looks round, the new furrow becomes crooked."

50. According to Jeremias, *New Testament Theology,* p. 33, "to enter" used with the Kingdom of God has no parallel outside the New Testament.

51. *Jesus and the Language,* p. 54.

52. As summarized by Perrin, *The Kingdom of God in the Teaching of Jesus* (London: SCM Press, 1963), p. 24. Gustaf Dalman's *Die Worte Jesu* was published in 1898 and translated by D. N. Day (Edinburgh: T. and T. Clarke, 1902). Perrin's reference is to pp. 91–93. See also the excellent discussion of Hermann Kleinknecht, Gerhard von Rad, Karl Kuhn, and K. L. Schmidt, *"Basileus," TDNT,* 1:564ff. esp. 580, and Jean Carmignac, *Le Mirage de L'Eschatologie: Royauté Règne et Royaume de Dieu* (Paris: Letouzey et Ane, 1979).

53. W. G. Kümmel, *Promise and Fulfillment,* trans. Dorothea M. Barton, Studies in Biblical Theology 23 (London: SCM Press, 1957), deals with the literature up to the mid-1950s. All three of Perrin's major works have dealt with these sayings.

54. *HST,* p. 14; Kümmel, *Promise and Fulfillment,* p. 105; Perrin, *Rediscovering,* p. 64, all agree that the present context of the saying is secondary and that this is an authentic Jesus saying.

55. E.g., Kümmel, *Promise and Fulfillment,* p. 106.

56. Blass and Debrunner, *A Greek Grammar of the New Testament,* hereinafter *BDF,* trans. Robert Funk (Chicago: University of Chicago Press, 1961), no. 105, p. 55.

57. *Jesus and the Language,* p. 43.

58. Kümmel, *Promise and Fulfillment,* p. 106, n. 3.

59. Perrin's most thorough discussion is to be found in *Rediscovering*, pp. 66–67. He is following a suggestion of T. W. Manson, *The Teaching of Jesus* (Cambridge: University Press, 1935), p. 82.

60. In English translations this is 8:19; in the Hebrew text 8:15.

61. Quoted by Perrin, *Rediscovering*, p. 66.

62. Ibid., p. 67.

63. *BDF*, no. 371, (1).

64. Perrin, *Rediscovering*, p. 67, would seem to be arguing in such a fashion.

65. The converse is also true—if they decide the casting out of demons is *not* the finger of God, then the Kingdom has not come.

66. Adolf von Harnack, *What is Christianity?* trans. Thomas Bailey Saunders (New York: Harper and Row Torchbooks, 1957).

67. *BAG*, p. 269, shows a definite preference for "within." Although Bauer refers to Xenophon as an example of *entos*, meaning "among," he doubts its relevance. Kümmel, *Promise and Fulfillment*, p. 33, n. 50, gives full evidence for both meanings.

68. Matt. 23:26, "You blind Pharisee! first cleanse the inside of the cup and of the plate, that the outside also may be clean."

69. Cf., Perrin, *Rediscovering*, p. 73. While it is beyond the scope of this study, I wonder whether the Aramaic presupposition can be maintained any longer. Galilee was bilingual. The possibility that some authentic Jesus sayings were originally in Greek and not translated from Aramaic merits careful study.

70. Kurt Aland, *Synopsis Quattuor Evangeliorum* (Stuttgart: Württembergische Bibelanstalt, 1964), p. 315. At this point in the text the words immediately following are missing; Fitzmyer has reconstructed them on the basis of Thomas.

71. Kümmel, *Promise and Fulfillment*, pp. 32–35. Since his argument has been very influential, I will summarize it closely.

72. Perrin, *Rediscovering*, p. 72 (also, *Kingdom of God*, p. 76), sees in this saying a rejection of apocalyptic speculation. Most apocalyptic speculation does not concern the coming of the Kingdom, but the turning of the aeons.

73. *Promise and Fulfillment*, p. 33.

74. Ibid., p. 34.

75. *Rediscovering*, p. 74.

76. In the Greek there is even a phonetic parallelism between the introductions to the two negative clauses:

ouk   erchetai
oude erousin

77. *"Biazomai,"* TDNT 1:609–13. Both Kümmel, *Promise and Fulfillment*, p. 122, and Perrin, *Kingdom of God*, p. 172, recognize the importance of Schrenk's article and adopt his arguments for the translation of *biazetai*. Quotes in the following discussion come from Schrenk unless otherwise noted.

78. BAG, p. 140: "nearly always as a middle."

79. Perrin, *Kingdom of God*, p. 172.

80. In the Lucan parallel, 16:16, *biazetai* must be understood as a middle; but the saying in Luke is his own construction.

81. The repetitive phonetic pattern of *biazetai kai biastai* is, as we have seen, characteristic of Jesus' sayings.

82. *Revue de Qumran* 6 (1967):89–107. Betz's article is more suggestive than convincing. He confuses Luke 16:16 with the Matthean saying, apparently assuming that both sayings are authentic. Some of his parallels likewise seem strained.

83. Ibid., pp. 100–101. Betz quotes a number of Rabbinic and Qumran texts to show this.

84. Ibid., pp. 95–98, for a large number of examples.

85. The LXX is only making explicit what is implied in the Massoretic text v. 24 but explicit in v. 21.

86. "The Problem of the Historical Jesus," *Essays on New Testament Themes*, trans. W. J. Montague, Studies in Biblical Theology 41 (London: SCM Press, 1964), p. 13. Cf. James M. Robinson, *A New Quest of the Historical Jesus*, Studies in Biblical Theology 25 (London: SCM Press, 1959), pp. 116ff.; Perrin, *Rediscovering*, pp. 76–77, quotes both with approval.

87. *The Prayers of Jesus*, trans. John Reumann, Studies in Biblical Theology 6 (London: SCM Press, 1967), p. 94. Jeremias's work is so widely available and accepted that there is no real point in repeating his arguments for the reconstruction of the prayer.

88. Ibid., p. 98; Perrin, *Jesus and the Language*, p. 47.

89. "Abba" in ibid., pp. 9–65; also "The Lord's Prayer in the Light of Recent Research," ibid., pp. 95ff. A convenient summary of Jeremias's position can be found in *New Testament Theology*, pp. 61–68.

90. *An Outline of the Theology of the New Testament*, trans. John Bowden (New York: Harper and Row, 1969), p. 103.

91. Perrin, *Rediscovering*, pp. 41–49, uses the criterion of dissimilarity in a convincing manner in this case.

92. Ibid., pp. 160–61.

93. Which is what it may mean for Perrin, e.g., *Jesus and the Language*, p. 43, where he refers to exorcisms as personally experienced reality because an individual is healed.

94. Jeremias, *The Prayers of Jesus*, pp. 91–93, 100–104. H. Bourgoin, *"Epiousios* expliqué par la notion de préfixe vide." *Biblica* 60 (1979): 91–96.

95. Ibid., pp. 105–6.

96. The problem is even further complicated in that there is no reliable outline in which to place these events, so a progression is not possible.

97. Gerd Theissen, *Urchistliche Wundergeschichten* (Gütersloh: Gütersloher Verlagshaus Gerd Mohn, 1974) is a promising beginning. *Semeia* 11 contains an important review of this work by Paul Achtemeier and Hendrikus Boers.

98. Paul Achtemeier's study "Miracles and the Historical Jesus: Mark 9:14–29," *Catholic Biblical Quarterly*, hereinafter *CBQ*, 37 (1975):471–91, provides an excellent example of the problems involved. After a very careful analysis of redaction and tradition, Achtemeier discovers "two miracle stories, one more easily removable than the other which, in their original form, it would appear circulated without specific interpretation" (p. 482). See also the important concluding paragraphs on p. 490. We are left, following Achtemeier's analysis, with the historic fact that Jesus was a wonder worker and was accepted as such by his contemporaries.

99. Geza Vermes, *Jesus the Jew* (London: Fontana/Collins, 1976; Philadelphia: Fortress Press, 1981) offers a number of promising suggestions for understanding Jesus' wonder-working activity in an historical context. Unfortunately the book is marred by serious methodological flaws.

100. Jeremias, *New Testament Theology*, pp. 109–10, shows that "sinners" is a stereotyped expression for a variety of people. For an important survey of the evidence, John R. Donahue, "Tax Collectors and Sinners: An Attempt at Identification," *CBQ* 33 (1971): 39–61. Wm. O. Walker, "Jesus and the Tax Collectors," *JBL* 97 (1978): 221–38, argues against Jesus' association with tax collectors.

101. Ibid., p. 112.

102. E.g., Matt. 11:18–19, where John as an ascetic is contrasted with Jesus the glutton and drunkard who associates with tax collectors and sinners. This saying seems to fulfill the negative criterion except for the Son of Man title. The linguistic problems associated with this title remain unsolved.

103. It is interesting that John omits association with the publicans.

104. Otto Michel, "telōnēs," *TDNT* 8: 105.

105. In the listing of the Twelve there is at least one zealot and one

publican, a very volatile situation; cf. Jeremias, *New Testament Theology*, p. 232.

106. Perrin, *Rediscovering*, p. 103, suggests that table fellowship was the primary provocative act in determining the need for his death.

107. Even though the Pharisees are represented in the Gospels as the primary group in opposition, it is not fair historically to single them out. Jesus sides with the '*am ha-aretz* against the more established forms of Judaism.

108. This is true of any established group.

109. This commonality of Jesus and Judaism and their essential symbolic unity is meant emphatically to disassociate my position from that of Ernst Käsemann, "The Problem of the Historical Jesus," in *Essays on New Testament Themes*, p. 38. "He cannot be integrated into the background of the Jewish piety of his time . . . he shatters this framework with his claim." But, of course, Jesus makes sense only in his Jewish framework.

6

EPILOGUE:
SYMBOL REVISITED

In this study we have accentuated the literary character of Jesus' language. His parables are artistic creations with beauty of structure and form;[1] other forms of his language exhibit these same characteristics. The recognition of this literary accent by modern American New Testament scholarship owes a debt to the pioneering work of Amos Wilder.[2] Others have followed his lead; the work of Funk and Crossan comes immediately to mind.[3]

But Jesus was not an artist in the self-consciously modern sense; he was not by trade a wordsmith. He was not literary in the written sense at all, for his culture was oral. It may be that Jesus' sophistication with oral forms derives in part from his culture's total reliance upon speech to communicate, the graphic arts for the most part being absent. The aural prominence appears in the floating logion: "He who has ears to hear, let him hear" (Mark 4:9). This proverb, which frequently recurs in the synoptic Gospels as an admonition, is quite paradoxical since it assumes the listener is deaf. It is a cry of frustration at the ear's refusal to perform its real task. We would say, "Why can't you see?" The difference between our visual and their aural model needs to be remembered.

But another difference between Jesus' language and literary language is even more frightening. It cost him his life. Nils Dahl's warning is to the point: any historical understanding of the ministry and message of Jesus must make sense of the fact

165

that that ministry ended on the cross.[4] We have dealt implicitly with this. The World implied in Jesus' vision of Kingdom is counter-World, a counter-World of blasphemy, not absurdity. He burlesques and pokes fun; his images are daring and at times scandalously inappropriate. But he should not be interpreted as being caught in the absurdity and insanity of modernity. The healing power of his images was what was terrifying to his opponents, and therefore they perceived him as demonic.

But we need to consider more than Jesus' death. James M. Robinson has shown that an exclusive concentration on logia, sayings, led in the ancient church to gnosticism.[5] Mark's incorporation of sayings into the larger form Gospel stunted the growth of the Wisdom trajectory.[6] This was accomplished not only by placing Jesus' death at the center, but also by arguing that it was Jesus of Nazareth who is risen (Mark 16:6). The period of revelation becomes the time prior to the resurrection, thereby making the death and resurrection the culmination of the Gospel's revelation. A historian who would be faithful to the claims of the material must ask if Jesus' language demands this interpretative framework. I am not concerned about attempting to verify the resurrection historically; such an attempt I would consider illegitimate. But does Jesus' language support the tradition's contention that apart from the death and resurrection his words are interpreted inauthentically?

A second observation also raises such a question. Among Jesus' audience there was a group that accepted his language, a group for whom it did not cause offense, but liberation and healing. From them came those who proclaimed his resurrection. Inevitably we must ask why they chose to believe that he had risen. Was there anything in his language that forecast their proclamation? To take seriously those who preserved his language demands that we investigate their claims. To rephrase, our question is impelled by two observations concerning the historical tradition of Jesus' sayings: (1) the affirmation that the correct hermeneutical context is his death and resurrection; (2) and that among those to whom his language was addressed was a group who proclaimed him as risen. If our analysis of Jesus' language is correct, then in that language they experienced the Kingdom of God. Therefore, their proclamation of his resurrection becomes an acute problem. How does their experience of Kingdom in his language relate to their proclamation of him as raised?

The experience of Kingdom in Jesus' language returns us to the point where we began our study. We accepted initially Norman Perrin's suggestion that in Jesus' language Kingdom of God was a tensive symbol. Perrin's own studies on Kingdom led us to conclude that scholarship's identification of Kingdom with the apocalyptic new aeon had led both to a misunderstanding of Kingdom language and to questions that were inappropriate. Several times we have seen that such an identification has caused a misreading of a parable or saying. By adopting as a hypothesis the tensive, symbolic character of Kingdom, we argued that its diachronic heritage did not determine its synchronic usage. We identified the parables as a synchronic system, and used an analysis of them to develop a model by which to examine other elements of the Jesus tradition. From that examination we have seen that his language is consistently tensive. Furthermore, it can be represented by a single generative model. Perrin's suggestion has allowed us to look at Jesus' language as a unified system of signs. Now we must turn our attention back to that to which the language refers, Kingdom of God, a symbol which refers to something unspoken.

Philip Wheelwright defines a symbol as "a relatively stable and repeatable element of perceptual experience, standing for some larger meaning or set of meanings which cannot be given, or not fully given, in perceptual experience itself."[7] This definition furnishes a starting point from which to understand how Kingdom is a symbol.

Given New Testament critics' overwhelming attention to Kingdom of God, we ought to remind ourselves that a symbol does not exist for itself or in itself. A symbol is a means of communicating from a sender to a receiver, but it is not an avenue into the sender's or the receiver's mind. It bridges the two, meaningful in its drawing both together. The basic communications model recalls this.[8]

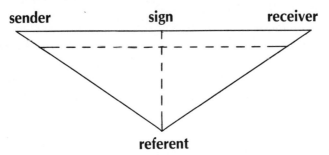

In any communication event there is an assumed commonality among all the terms. If there were none, communication would be impossible.

A symbol is an element of perceptual experience. It both results from perception and attempts to create a perspective by which a Receiver can perceive the Referent. To do this, Sender selects and organizes images in the symbol so that a particular aspect of reality is refracted for the Receiver. Kingdom of God as a symbol creates a perspective from (or by) which to view its Referent. From all the possible ways of categorizing its Referent, a Sender has selected this particular symbol. This demands attention to the economy of the symbol. For the symbol Kingdom of God, the referential perspective is God exercising kingship.

Creating perspective is characteristic of symbolic language. Wheelwright has employed the helpful distinction between steno- and tensive language. In steno-language meanings "can be shared in exactly the same way by a very large number of persons."[9] Such language is common everyday language with its guaranteed, assured meaning. The perspective is the commonly shared, everyday experience of the world about us. Tensive language is conflictive, consciously aware that it does not maintain an exact correlation to its referent. The conflictive, tensive element potentially discloses deeper meanings in what is.[10] Tensive and steno-language are not either/or options in language. Tensive language is always somewhat steno, or otherwise there would be no basis for communication.[11]

Whether language is tensive or steno depends both upon the Sender's perception of the Referent (object) as well as upon the referent itself. Objects which are not part of everyday life, that belong to the deeper dimensions of life, demand the use of tensive language to be heard. We hear such meanings in the cracks between a sign's everyday meaning and the tensive experience of the referent. Tensive language both "creates and discloses certain hitherto unknown, unguessed aspects of what is."[12]

Because a symbol has tensive possibilities, it is "a relatively stable and repeatable element of perceptual experience." Relative stability grants a symbol independence from both sender and receiver. While an artist has creative intentions in the use of a symbol, it must nevertheless be relatively stable to be tensive. At first these two requirements seem contradictory—how can something stable be tensive? But stability results from a symbol's heritage, or diachronic structure, while tensiveness concerns its relation to a referent. Kingdom of God's stability as symbol derives from its usage in Israel's language stock, as well as from the very stability of the words themselves. The words "Kingdom" and "God" are stable referents. But a sender can intensify the relation between symbol and referent. He will indicate through the symbol's mimetic possibilities that the relation is tensive.

Kingdom's stability as symbol is both its weakness and its strength. As a stable symbol it can, as Perrin has pointed out, refer to Israel's past.[13] It has a richness and a depth of linguistic signification referring to God's past actions as King. This involves the inevitable images associated with kingship—ruling, majesty, empire, power—but also the peculiar images of Israel's history of kingship—David and his successors. There is further the story of the division and loss of kingdom and the promise of its restoration, the failure and repentance of the people and foreign domination and repression. All of these, plus many more, are part of the imaginative associations that make up the symbol's stability and potential for meaning. Historical criticism's fruitless search for a specific meaning for the phrase is based on the false premise that it was a steno-symbol. Had it been a steno-symbol, it would not have been available to Jesus because it would have lacked semantic potential.[14]

According to Wheelwright, tensive language has two meta-phorical models. Epiphora is the normal mode of comparative relationship: A is like B because there is something that A and B share in common. The semantic movement (*phora*) is from the more commonly known to the unknown. Diaphoric metaphor is semantic movement "through certain particulars of experience (actual or imagined) in a fresh way, producing new meaning by juxtaposition alone."[15] Diaphoric metaphor depends upon the unexpected comparison of the supposedly non-comparable. This creates a powerful metaphor that generates the referent's presence. By combining known elements in new ways, fissures are created in the impenetrable facade of mystery. For Wheel-wright there are no pure diaphoric symbols, "for wherever any imitative or mimetic factor is present, whether in imitation of nature or of previous art or a mimesis of some recognizable idea, there is an element of epiphor."[16] Were there no relation of epiphor, there could be no possible relation between sign and referent. Thus, in the best symbols, diaphor and epiphor work in combination.

Metaphorical language has a tendency to create a semantic overload; it "tends toward semantic plentitude, rather than to-ward a cautious semantic economy."[17] This overload is once again due to the referent. Wheelwright describes this in terms of vehicle and tenor: "the one for the imagery or concrete situation described, the other for the ulterior significance that this sug-gests to the responsive imagination."[18] This distinction has the advantage of firmly suggesting metaphor's non-literal, transitory, stand-in character and its resonating impact on the imagination. Kingdom of God is a vehicle whose tenor is greater than what the words suggest. It is this "greater than" that creates the se-mantic overload.

In Jesus' language an analysis of the symbol Kingdom of God is complicated because (1) it is a vehicle for an unexpressed tenor, and (2) it is an expressed tenor for the vehicle parable. Further the various forms of Jesus' language are metaphoric, or better, tensive, frequently compounded tensive language creat-ing intense semantic plentitude. This is precisely why it is dif-ficult, perhaps even impossible, to state what Jesus meant.

There is no single interpretation of his language. Its semantic potential will play variously upon the receiver's imagination.

When Jesus chose Kingdom as symbol for the tenor he wanted to communicate, he faced an immediate problem: he had to judge whether the symbol as constituted was adequate for his referent. Just because the symbol was chosen should not lead us into a determinism; the choice was arbitrary.[19] But once made, we must assume that it was chosen because of an element of similarity—of available linguistic symbols that mimic the experience, this one is the most adequate. Or to rephrase: the sender judges the epiphoric openness of the symbol as containing the potential for permitting the receiver to experience the referent. As epiphor, a symbol operates much like a filter by narrowing and selecting aspects of images that will act as filters which allow through the authenticated experience. This enables the sender and the receiver to guarantee a ground of communication.

But because Kingdom is a tensive symbol, its filter resembles a sieve. Semantic potential needs room for development, for conflict between the imaginative suggestions of sign and referent. Without this broadness, looseness, and potential it would be a steno-symbol. Because symbol is perspectival, Jesus must create a language about the symbol to focus the perspective. For this reason Jesus' tensive language provides a perspective, referential nexus, for the symbol. His tensive language provides a metaphorical vehicle, creating or increasing the potential for meaning of the tenor, Kingdom of God.

In chapters 2, 3, and 5 selected forms of the Jesus tradition were examined in an effort to sketch in discursive language and represent with a generative model (chapter 4) the outlines of that perspective or referential nexus. Because tensive language generates this perspective, discursive language cannot replace it. The discussion about Jesus' language must never replace the language itself. To do so would violate the critic's responsibility to help a reader appreciate the language. Nevertheless the critic can describe how that language achieves its goals or purposes.

When Jesus moves beyond the broadest filtering possibilities of his chosen symbol, he does so because (1) he has detected something different about the referent than is normally implied in the symbol, and (2) has seen other potentialities in the symbol itself. There are two ways open to express this difference. He can combine the epiphors in a variety of new ways and/or he can introduce diaphor. Actually he does both. In analyzing this aspect of Jesus' language watertight categories are impossible.

Examples of simple epiphor in Jesus' language are infrequent since, as we shall see, much of his symbolic usage is diaphoric. His frequent use of Old Testament references has not always been recognized, but we have seen how frequently they do appear. "Finger of God" in the saying about the casting out of demons uses Yahweh's deliverance of his people from Pharaoh's power as an epiphor to interpret Jesus' exorcisms. In A Great Banquet there is probably an epiphoric reference to the Messianic banquet. Even though the parabolic banquet parodies the Messianic one, nevertheless it is an epiphor for Kingdom. A more prominent use of epiphor occurs in A Father Had Two Sons. A two-sons tradition is part of Israel's folklore and has been used in the self-understanding of Israel. The parable's retelling of that tradition is epiphoric. Not only is the two-sons tradition part of Israel's self-understanding but characters in the parable undoubtedly have epiphoric references. The father is not God, nor is the younger son Israel nor the elder Esau, but they participate in these larger sets of meanings. Part of a symbol's tensive overload is its ability to suggest imaginatively more than one referent. The logic of symbols is determined by imaginative associations, not rules of discourse.

Common in the Jesus tradition is the combination of epiphor and diaphor. The Mustard Plant is such a combination. Mustard seed by itself contains the epiphoric possibility of contrast (Mark's tradition developed this), but as it unfolds the metaphor becomes diaphoric. The true epiphor is the implicit Great Tree referred to in the last line. When the mustard plant in its ordinariness becomes a metaphor for Kingdom, then the symbol is effected by the diaphoric conflict between the mustard seed's imaginative power and the expected image (Great Tree) for the named referent. The normal associative images of Kingdom (power, might, majesty) are juxtaposed against the associative images of a mustard plant (smallness, insignificance). The parable abandons the epiphoric possibilities (growth from smallness) for diaphoric possibilities (insignificance). The parable forms a perspective for viewing the referent, Kingdom. The diaphor makes the referent present in that moment when the Great Tree in its majesty is abandoned for the insignificant mustard plant— in that diaphoric insight Kingdom of God is present.[20]

Two examples from the sayings tradition may also be used to exhibit this combination. Luke 17:21, concerning the Kingdom's coming, appeals epiphorically to both the common-sense meaning of Kingdom and the apocalyptic imagery associated with it. But the epiphoric appeal (not with signs, not here or there) is replaced by diaphor: it is in your midst. The apparent absence of signs and place is affirmed as presence, creating a diaphoric juxtaposition. Likewise Matt. 11:12 makes an epiphoric reference to the Sinai tradition only to reverse the reference diaphorically. The Sinai tradition occurs in two ways: (1) Kingdom itself is breaking out, and (2) violent men attack it (which may be an epiphoric reference to apocalyptic violence). These two epiphors are applied to Jesus' present activity, which surely is diaphoric from the receiver's viewpoint. When taken together these two sayings constitute clear proof of both the tensive and symbolic character of Kingdom of God in Jesus' language. How can something be neither observed nor pointed to, have been since the days of John the Baptist, attack and be attacked, and yet be *entos* (within and in your midst)? How can it be historical (the Kingdom is clearly historical) and not be calculated or demarcated? Such juxtaposition creates a powerful diaphoric impact upon the imagination, and that impact is Kingdom—pure presence!

Examples of intense diaphor are common in the Jesus tradition. The proverb "Let the dead bury the dead," while not absurdist, is diaphoric in its unexpected and sarcastic juxtaposition within the imagination, which forces the receiver to surrender everyday moorings. The juxtaposition also jars loose the Kingdom's epiphoric anchors and reconstructs them as diaphor.

The parables of Leaven and Jerusalem to Jericho are also examples of intense diaphoric imagery. Leaven itself is a diaphor for Kingdom and creates a negative juxtaposition upon the receiver's consciousness. As the presiding image it creates an overall negative impact. The second parable achieves a diaphoric effect with the introduction of a negative character in a positive role: Samaritan as savior of Jew.

The Fig Tree may be one of the purest forms of diaphor imaginable. "From the fig tree learn its parable" promises a parable, that is, it promises the fig tree will stand for something else. "As soon as its branch becomes tender and puts forth its leaves, you know that summer is near." But the promised parable disappears. It is parable because it is not parable, diaphorically juxtaposing the normal description of a budding fig tree as a sign for summer's coming for an expected parable. Formally, this is an experiment in parable, testing how far form can be pushed and still remain a parable. Perhaps it is best seen as a metaparable, a parable about parables.[21]

These metaphorical vehicles for the symbol Kingdom of God, both in their epiphoric and diaphoric modes, heighten tensiveness. The greater tensiveness also heightens the mimetic possibilities by creating a greater impression of the referent's presence. This new language and reorganization of images recontextualizes the symbol Kingdom of God, focusing an experience of the referent that is new, different, unexpected from the normal representation.

This new context (referential nexus, perspective) surfaced in the generative model. That model was set up in binary terms because meaning results from associations: between sender and receiver, symbol and referent. There is no meaning isolated from these dialectical relations. Jesus' vision of Kingdom is possible only as seen with and against other visions of Kingdom.

The symbol's dialectical associations and mimetic possibility raise the question of judgment. There are two different poles of judgment in the communications model. The sender must judge the adequacy of sign to referent, which determines his performance, and the receiver must judge the sender's alignment of sign to referent. In diaphoric language judgment is problematic since the operation is one of juxtaposition and not similarity. In any metaphor such a dual judgment by sender and receiver is required. One can after all decide that the metaphor does not work.

In Jesus' language judgment presents a special problematic. The referent of the symbol Kingdom of God is an ultimate who makes ultimate claims upon human experience. Because Jesus' language is tensive, it claims to disclose the ultimate in a new way. For the sender, the referent's ultimacy demands or implies a relation with that ultimate sufficient to generate the symbol. In Jesus' language, which so often is culturally dissonant, an added strain is placed upon the implied relationship. The presence of the referent in metaphor must generate the strength of conviction, a conviction of the language's adequacy and the inadequacy of normal ways of symbolizing the referent.

Jesus' parables imply a relation to Yahweh, which furthermore is present within his sayings. The sender has judged that the symbols of Exodus and Sinai can be applied to what is happening in his experience. This implies a decision on Jesus' part about his relation to Yahweh and represents a claim about his relation to Yahweh. One need not develop or categorize the claim, but the claim is impicit within the symbol.

The receiver's situation also involves judgment. In the mimetic moment when the receiver experiences the referent's presence, one decides whether the symbol really presents its intended referent. Is the experience granted in the symbol truly the referent? In the Jesus tradition the rejection of the symbol as revealing ultimate reality gave rise to the accusation that he was in league with demons. Both sides agree that the symbol exposed the ultimate, but for one it was a demonic ultimate.

The one who acknowledges the referent as divine has faith in the exposed ultimate. In symbol one has met the ultimate. In Jesus' language, the ultimate shatters the receiver's everyday World, categorizing it as Illusion, and creating a new World in a new perspective. For the receiver, World truly ends. The contraries of the generative model constrain the contours of that World. We need not repeat our analysis here. Ultimately, it may be so simple as to say that Jesus' referent represents a radical restoration of the first commandment: the creator claiming his creation.[22] Nothing can stand as god over against Yahweh, so that the experience of the Kingdom heals tragedy by incorporating it into the Kingdom's life. We have shown over and over again that underlying Jesus' language are themes of unity—not absorption into oneness, but a unity of having been claimed. Powerful symbolic divisions are held together in his language.

> A father had two sons
> It is not here; it is not there; it is in your midst
> Let the dead bury the dead
> Thy Kingdom come; from the days of John the Baptist
> If by the finger of God; leaven

In his language what appear to be contraries are not organized into opposites but held together by a third, unspoken reality. The ultimate to which parables refer claims the receiver. Whoever judges the symbol to present the referent has experienced an ultimate claim upon existence; that one has faith in the one true God of Israel through a restored vision of that God.

This brings us back to our original question, the faith of the disciples. Three implications of Jesus' language bear upon this: (1) Jesus' language implies faith in a restored vision of Yahweh. In this sense his mission was prophetic. (2) His language implies claims about his own relation to Yahweh. The teller of parables and the exorcist makes direct claims about his ability to focus the real. (3) His language implies or points to a future. It is tensive, plurisignificant, open-ended language. By creating a new perspective, a new World, it recontextualizes what is. That in itself demands a future.

This perspectival World generated the language of the primitive confession of resurrection. This is to say, the initial language of resurrection is understandable within the generative model of Jesus' language. The primitive kerygma acknowledged that Jesus was raised (*egēgertai*).[23] The language, borrowed from traditional Jewish notions for the final act of Yahweh, symbolizes the reality the original group experienced after Jesus' death.[24] "He was raised" is a symbol referring to a referent whose characteristic is that God has restored Jesus to life. By continuity of perspective and by the demand for faith Jesus' language generates the language of resurrection.

His language creates for its receiver a perspective that impels faith—explicitly a faith in Yahweh and implicitly a faith in the sender as a symbol-maker for Yahweh. The presiding symbol of the perspective is Kingdom of God. For the one who believes that the symbol makes Yahweh present, Reality is different—previous reality was Illusion. But in the perspective of this new Reality (Kingdom), Comedy appears as Tragedy, the ordinary ordering of affairs (Status) surrenders to Reality filled with Grace and Wholeness, and Reality is grasped from the outside. Faith, as a primary relation in this vision, rejects Ideology as a way of relating. In this we come to the crux of the problem. To believe in Jesus' World one must surrender the Ideology's predictability for Faith. The examples we have seen of faith do not demand an abandonment, a leap in the night, but right judgment about what is, which is made possible by the symbol's creating openness. Ideology blocks judgment by obscuring symbolic presence.

This World which makes faith possible graces the receiver with a new Reality symbolized in Jesus' language. Because of faith in Jesus' World, the original group could see by insight the referent of resurrection as making sense of Jesus. God's raising Jesus from the dead makes sense in such a World. In a World where World has ended, to be raised up by God is the *logical* consequence of the death on the cross—the Comic appears under the guise of Tragedy. God's destruction of death in Jesus' death destroys the ultimate division of Reality and shows forth this new Reality as the presence of Grace. Belief in the resurrection and belief in Jesus' World are dialectically related. Belief in the resurrection is made possible by the perspective of Jesus' World and the symbol of that referent is congruent with the symbol of Jesus' World.

NOTES

1. Dan O. Via, *The Parables* (Philadelphia: Fortress Press, 1967), chap. 3, has defined parables as aesthetic objects.

2. Amos Wilder, *Early Christian Rhetoric: The Language of the Gospel* (Cambridge: Harvard University Press, 1st ed., 1964); this interest has run throughout the work of Wilder.

3. Robert Funk, *Jesus as Precursor*, Semeia Studies (Philadelphia: Fortress Press: Missoula, Mont.: Scholars Press, 1975); John Dominic Crossan, *Raid on the Articulate: Comic Eschatology in Jesus and Borges* (New York: Harper and Row, 1976).

4. "The Problem of the Historical Jesus," in *The Crucified Messiah* (Minneapolis: Augsburg Publishing House, 1974), pp. 72ff.

5. "*LOGOI SOPHON: On the Gattung of Q*," with Helmut Koester, in *Trajectories through Early Christianity* (Philadelphia: Fortress Press, 1971), esp. pp. 112ff.

6. Helmut Koester, "One Jesus and Four Primitive Gospels," ibid., p. 161; for a thorough discussion of gospel as an interpretative context see Leander Keck, *A Future for the Historical Jesus* (1971; reprint ed., Philadelphia: Fortress Press, 1981), chap. 3.

7. Philip Wheelwright, *Metaphor and Reality* (Bloomington: Indiana University Press, 1962, Midland Book Edition, 1968), p. 92.

8. This model is the one used by Susan Wittig, "A Theory of Multiple Meanings," *Semeia* 9 (1977): 79.

9. *Metaphor and Reality*, p. 33.

10. Wheelwright's distinction is similar to one Funk has made between sedimented and refracted language (*Jesus as Precursor*, pp. 57ff.).

11. Steno-language is also tensive and never as assured as it seems, because the relation between Signifier and Signified is arbitrary, thus creating the potential for conflict. Wheelwright's example of a steno-symbol, the mathematical symbol *pi*, itself represents an unexpressible number.

12. *Metaphor and Reality*, p. 51.

13. Perrin, *Jesus and the Language of the Kingdom* (Philadelphia: Fortress Press, 1976), pp. 16–32.

14. Perrin, ibid., pp. 30–32, argues that Kingdom of God in Judaism is both a steno- and tensive symbol. I think this simply confuses the point. Even if it does predominantly refer to the apocalyptic coming of a new aeon, this is hardly a steno reality. See the helpful critique of Perrin in Earl Breech, "Kingdom of God and the Parables of Jesus," *Semeia* 12 (1978): 25–26.

15. *Metaphor and Reality*, p. 78.

16. Ibid., p. 79.

17. Ibid., p. 57.

18. Ibid., p. 55.

19. This is to remind us of the fundamental distinction made by Ferdinand de Saussure, *Course in General Linguistics*, trans. Wade

Baskin (New York: Philosophical Library, 1959), p. 67, that the relation between the signifier and signified is arbitrary.

20. This same pattern could be worked out for each parable. There is in each a moment of abandonment when the Kingdom of God is present. This moment is parallel to what has traditionally been called revelation.

21. John Dominic Crossan would seem to be arguing that all of Jesus' parables are metaparables, see *Finding Is the First Act*, Semeia Studies (Missoula, Mont.: Scholars Press and Philadelphia: Fortress Press, 1979), esp. p. 120.

22. A phrase used by Ernst Käsemann, *Jesus Means Freedom*, trans. Frank Clark (Philadelphia: Fortress Press, 1972), p. 31.

23. See the discussion of Reginald Fuller, *The Formation of the Resurrection Narratives* (1971; reprint ed., Philadelphia: Fortress Press, 1980), pp. 17–23. John Klopenborg, "An Analysis of the Pre-Pauline Formula in I Cor. 15:3b–5 in Light of Some Recent Literature," *Catholic Biblical Quarterly* 40 (1978): 362–63, sees the antithesis "he died/was raised" as the most primitive unit behind the formula of 1 Cor. 15:3b–5.

24. Our concern is not to prove what happened, but to trace the *semantic* relations between Jesus' language and this kerygmatic formula.

INDEX

BIBLICAL REFERENCES

AUTHORS